D0826617

Today You Are My Favorite Poet

Donated by
MA English Department
2014

Today You Are My Favorite Poet

WRITING POEMS WITH TEENAGERS

Geof Hewitt

HEINEMANN
Portsmouth, NH

Heinemann
A division of Reed Elsevier Inc.
361 Hanover Street
Portsmouth, NH 03801–3912
http://www.heinemann.com

Offices and agents throughout the world

The author and publisher wish to thank those who have generously given permission to reprint borrowed material:

"Haiku" by Ron Padgett. From *New & Selected Poems* by Ron Padgett. Reprinted by permission of David R. Godine, Publisher, Inc. Copyright © 1995 by Ron Padgett.

"Parents" from *Search for the New Land* by Julius Lester. Copyright © 1969 by Julius Lester. Used by permission of The Dial Press/Dell Publishing, a division of Bantam Doubleday Dell Publishing Group, Inc.

Excerpt from "Asphodel, That Greeny Flower" by William Carlos Williams. From *Collected Poems 1939–1962, Volume II.* Copyright © 1944 by William Carlos Williams. Reprinted by permission of New Directions Publishing Corp.

"Ben Carries the Cracked Egg," "The Moon," "Comet Come," "Introduction," "Eagle Rock," "Passing Thru," "The Ruffed Grouse," "Recipe," "Wrestling to Lose," and "Moment" by Geof Hewitt originally appeared in *Just Worlds.* Copyright © 1989 by Geof Hewitt. Published by Ithaca House. Reprinted by permission of the author and publisher.

"Psyche" by Alfred Starr Hamilton originally appeared in *Sphinx.* Copyright © 1968 by The Kumquat Press. Reprinted by permission of the author.

Acknowledgments for borrowed materials continue on p. 130.

Library of Congress Cataloging-in-Publication Data
Hewitt, Geof.
    Today you are my favorite poet : writing poems with teenagers /
Geof Hewitt.
        p.   cm.
    Includes bibliographical references.
    ISBN 0–86709–452–4 (alk. paper)
    Poetry—Study and teaching (Secondary) 2. English language—
Composition and exercises. 3. Creative writing (Secondary
education). 4. Poetry—Authorship. I. Title.
PN1101.H46   1998
808.1—dc21
                                                              98-29643
                                                                  CIP

Editor: William Varner
Production: Vicki Kasabian
Cover design: Jenny Jensen Greenleaf
Manufacturing: Louise Richardson

Printed in the United States of America on acid-free paper
02 01 00 99 98   DA   1 2 3 4 5

Don't teach poetry. Share it.
  —Linda Rief, *Seeking Diversity*

Poetry is an art practised with the terribly plastic material of human language. . . . Poetry is the journal of a sea animal living on land, wanting to fly the air. . . . Poetry is a search for syllables to shoot at the barriers of the unknown and the unknowable. . . . Poetry is the capture of a picture, a song, or a flair, in a deliberate prism of words.
—Carl Sandburg, *Atlantic Monthly,* March 1923

> It is difficult
> to get the news from poems
> yet men die miserably every day
> for lack
> of what is found there.
>
> —William Carlos Williams,
> from "Asphodel, That Greeny Flower"

Contents

Acknowledgments

Unless otherwise indicated, sixth- through twelfth-grade students wrote the poems in this book. I am deeply grateful to them, and to their parents, for permission to publish this work. I also want to thank the adult poets who contributed their poems.

Joan Simmons and Bill Varner read early drafts of this book, and gave me excellent guidance. Joan, an eighth-grade teacher, kept at me to finish the project, telling me: "Hurry up! We *need* this book!"

Ron Padgett showed me the way out of a helpless tangle of ideas as I was revising my chapter on metaphor.

Just Another O'Connor Burgess Carter Major Production (Montpelier, Vermont), transformed my charts and diagrams into figures and drawings that I am proud to include.

My supervisors and colleagues at the Vermont Department of Education, Elaine Grainger, Doug Walker, Penny Bishop, Mary Ann Minardo, Sue Biggam, Rose Wheeler, and Allison Welch were patient, helpful, and understanding when I requested, then extended, a leave of absence to finish this project.

Claire Feldman thought she was done when she published a chapbook of poems. Her reflections on these poems, which start each chapter, offer a priceless look into the thoughts of a young poet.

Janet Lind Hewitt, thoughtful teacher and patient guide, helped in many ways, especially by reading what I thought was the final draft of this book, just enough days before the deadline that I could make the changes she suggested.

Introduction

Make It New!

Until I reached college in 1962, I was taught poetry wrong. Poetry was procrastinated. It was springtime's tack-on to tiring English classes, five weeks of reading small print from the back of a fat, foul-smelling, shiny-paper text followed by a week when the teacher let the students try to write their own poems.

What we now call a poet's strategies were presented as rules, and the content of poems came in three levels of meaning, the second and third the teacher's special secrets we could guess at and feel foolish about when we were, inevitably, wrong.

The focus of discussion was skewed toward technical matters, often represented by jargon (onomatopoeia, alliteration, iambic pentameter, personification) to memorize, and confusing methods of analysis. Take rhyme scheme: Describing poetic patterns alphabetically is an alienating tradition! Numbers, odd or even in a regular pattern, make a rhyme scheme easy to see. Letters, which are vowels or consonants in no regular pattern, make alphabetical annotations confusing once the rhymes surpass the letter *c.*

In countless other ways, poetry deserves to be demystified, so its power is evident to adults and young people alike.

A focus on technical considerations usurps the exploration of the issues behind a poem, and in my English classes (the only place the word *poetry* ever came up!) the attitude of the narrator, on the rare occasions it was acknowledged, was immediately linked to a technical matter in the phoniest of ways: "The narrator's anger is reinforced by the hissing sounds evident in the alliterative use of the letter *s*." In those days, teachers treated poetry with so much awe it was pretty clear that no living human could be as important as a great poem.

Certainly, the disgust or boredom or rare enthusiasm evident in student poems were never considered. The chance to snag students' interest in language became a springtime turnoff for teacher and student alike.

But that's the 1950s for you.

I vowed revenge, never imagining that it would involve teaching and writing, probably an instinctual attempt to undo the kind of shallow, distant teaching that kept young people in their place.

In this book I am presenting the attitudes and teaching strategies, the exercises and student responses, that have sweetened my experience, since 1970, as a writer and teacher of poem writing. Poetry is a tool every literate person should have, if only for the pleasure or therapeutic value of writing it. It served me so well during my teenage years that writing poems has become a lifelong source of pleasure. It has also been a modest source of income, well . . . during one or two of my *good* years; yet, indirectly, my habit of writing poems has led to a livelihood. It's worth smiling over the fact that something as fun and impractical as writing poems can lead to a livelihood!

Impractical? Maybe that depends on the poem or the person who's writing it. I think of poetry as a tool.

I also think of poetry as a nation. It's a land where every person has an equal chance for success. It's a place where, if you are blind, your ears and fingers, your nose, your own good brain and heart become eyes. If your disability is mental or emotional, you are still equipped for success in this marvelous land. Complete sentences are not required, a vocabulary of a few hundred words will suffice, and any form of human expression that can be represented two dimensionally or in braille or through utterance is accepted. Sophisticated language is welcome here, but so are chanting and song, patterns and repetitions of tone and sound and rhythm.

This is a place that can be totally private; no "authority figures" are lurking in the hall! Where better to express feelings and work out relationships than on paper? And here, too, is a way to display or perform or otherwise to make a public statement, to publish.

What a place for teenagers it is, but age makes no difference! Think of Ezra Pound's often-quoted "Make it new!" or his outburst, as quoted in Hayden Carruth's poem "Vermont," "Curiosity, gorbloastit, kuryossity— thass wot I'm tawkin about!" An eighty-year-old beginner has the same chance as a top-of-the-career expert, who is just as likely as a four-year-old to come up with something that works. A good poem is a good poem, no matter who composed it. Here's one by a four-year-old, merely given a title and transcribed, word for word, by a proud father, me.

Ben Carries the Cracked Egg

This one's for you, Geof,
I think they'll lay my egg tomorrow.

Because "the rules" of poetry writing encourage an infinite diversity of approaches, all our idiosyncrasies—any set of rules or limitations, even disabilities—can be made to work in our favor. French novelist George Perec wrote an entire novel, entitled *A Void*, avoiding all words that contain the letter *e*. Gilbert Adair translated it into English observing the same limitation; critics have noted that the language, in both the French and English editions, is strangely enhanced. In constraint, the poet uses language in new ways. Whether from naïveté, necessity, or sophisticated wordplay, a voice asserts itself, becoming a poet's style.

"Let your awkwardness work for you," is how David Ray, my first college-level creative-writing teacher, put it.

What differentiates the thirty-five-year-old career poet from the four-year-old neophyte may have more to do with ambition, persistence, a constant ear tuned to receive the moments of poetry that flash through one's consciousness, than with linguistic ability. The unselfconsciousness of a person newly using language is a strength our poor professional long ago lost. The "awkwardness" to which David Ray refers is that which is individual: a true rendering of one's being, one's personality, one's *voice!*

Children under the age of eighteen are in a constant state of newness; caring teachers, no matter how minimal their knowledge of poetry, can nurture a student's willingness to explore, in words, this constantly evolving state. Would a portfolio of poems, culled from a writer's first eighteen years, be more convincing to a college admissions office, prospective spouse, or potential employer than a transcript, a diamond ring, or a résumé? In Japan, the average high school graduate is said to have written more than one thousand haiku. Keep dipping into *that* well throughout your childhood and you're bound to pull up a few pails of liquid gold.

Writers of poetry respond to atmosphere more than to curriculum, and the best writing atmosphere is created when *everyone* (yes, the teacher, too!) writes. To increase students' odds of frequent success, offer quick daily opportunities for dipping into the well! The product is valued, but there is broad understanding that the *process* of writing is the long-term, ongoing habit we seek to honor. Aesthetic response should be balanced with talk about how the author created the work: a discussion, without judgment, of process—an appreciation of each writer's collection of strategies.

To kindle awareness of what poems can do—and this is the writing teacher's number one challenge, to break the straitjacket of stereotype: poetry as pretty language arranged in meter and rhyme—I recommend a good supply of short, short poems. Have students read ten or twelve at a clip, then ask each student to discuss a favorite with the rest of the class. Get hold of *Pocket Poems* (Janeczko 1985) or *Poems One Line & Longer* (Cole 1973) (see Bibliography), or some other anthology of short, short poems, and turn your students loose. For a mix of short and somewhat longer poems, see Naomi Shihab Nye's anthology of poems from around the world, *This Same Sky* (1992). For American poetry of the twentieth century, I recommend Hayden Carruth's comprehensive anthology, *The Voice That Is Great Within Us* (1996).

Another excellent resource is any of Dave Morice's *Poetry Comics* series, now in book-length collections (see Bibliography), but initially published as a periodical. *Poetry Comics* presents classic, modern, and contemporary poems in comic-book fashion, frame by frame, just as *Classics Illustrated* once did with the world's great novels. *Poetry Comics* reminds us that *the reader owns the poem*; it may be interpreted in all sorts of unexpected ways.

Without a forest of examples of short poems, each requiring a fraction of the time needed for longer poems, the student may never see through the awe or intimidation imposed by previous encounters with poetry. Reminding yourself and your students that there is no expectation that you'll like or appreciate every poem, note the names of authors whose work you *do* like and search out the books those authors have published.

The magic of only a few words, as in haiku or in brief free verse, can enchant a reader or an audience perhaps because of their simplicity or their seeming disregard for conventional English, as in many of Alfred Starr Hamilton's poems. I met Hamilton when I was still in college and found that he spoke with the same density of metaphor that infuses his poems; "literal" conversation was rare. Two of my favorite Hamilton poems are "Psyche" and "Town." Although I cannot deduce a literal meaning in "Psyche," its final three lines convey a sense of famine.

Psyche

but I don't know
however it felt more like
scraping one's spareribs
for what is left of
the moon at the bottom of the pan

Town

Give us time
Give us crickets
Give us a clock
could you build this wonderful town house in the grass
and put a cricket in it by this evening?

My concept of poetry allows everyone to play. A poem is language performed aloud with intentional effect or language on the page where the author, not a computer or typesetter, determines the placement of the words. Such a fundamental definition borders on excluding *poet* as a useful noun, since everyone who uses language with intentional effect is a poet. Accepting this notion, one's attention shifts from the author to the poem. The question is not "Am I a poet?" but "Is what I have written a poem?"

Working with teenagers, I often notice that questions of personal identity are more readily confronted in poetry than in other forms of expression. For starters, as I've already mentioned, it is private. Poetry also offers metaphor and symbolism and persona as traditions that encourage some young writers to explore personal or difficult themes. In those ways, poetry is an open invitation to emotional risk. And the author controls the extent to which the result is made public: It can always be destroyed.

So this book presents specific teaching and writing strategies and tells stories about the use of these strategies, with examples of student responses. Claire Feldman's poems, and her assessment of each poem, appear at the start of each chapter as a way of reminding the reader of the extraordinary variety of approaches and attitudes one teenage writer can use in writing poems. Feldman, now in college, wrote these poems as a high school student, over a period of three or four years, publishing them in a chapbook as part of her senior year project. With commentaries she wrote after she published her book, the poems cumulatively suggest the contents of a poetry portfolio, a collection of best work and analysis, or self-assessment, of that work.

The best poetry teachers are active participants in their writing workshops. Work created in their classrooms (their own and their students') is given the same respect as that written by "the masters." Maybe my saying this up front will make unnecessary the many little lectures I always want to give. Write with your students; let them know you're trying, too!

If you do that one thing, you'll learn more, and accomplish more, than you'll ever get by following even the most useful guide. This book can then supplement the best practice there is: Go do it yourself!

The Moon

What can be said for the moon above
The shimmering light that shone my love
How can I fly and touch thy beams
Far and wide what a distance it seems

Crescent or full enhances the sky
Hail the moon in the darkness though lie
A distance of brightness, naked thy shine
I dreamt of a vision that thou were mine

Tell me not that beauty lie soon
Only can I dream that thou art thy moon

▼

I really dislike this poem, it rhymes and sounds antique. It is the first poem I ever consciously wrote.

—*Claire Feldman*

1
Anatomy of a Poetry Workshop

As I write this chapter, I am halfway through a two-week residential summer arts institute for 120 high school students. I teach poetry writing here, two hours a day for twelve days, with Sunday off. From past experience I know how quickly these two weeks disappear, and the students with them. This summer I am frustrated by the fact that many of the students claim to *want* their poems vague. Where a subject or topic can be identified, it emerges from a small range of major issues: love and death, suicide and vampires, one-way friendships. Without outright statements, the poems of teenage writers often convey strong feeling and a sense of alienation. In the following poem, student Jessie Stewart balances alienation in the first twelve lines with a telling allusion to childhood, as expressed in the images and rhyme of the final five lines.

Ho-Jo's

We were the no goers
The no show HO-JO's
No time for the flashy plastic romance
Just our 4 mumble masses
VooDoo Board
Op.Ivy
Guitar
and pale midnight stars
Their congregating masses of Kings and Queens
Crowd their courts

Beauty Queen wanna-be's
Fakest of the fake
Our numbers being few
Caused us to remain quite true
No Glimmering Gown
To manipulate the unfound sound
That will break their crown

"There's no subject too small for poetry." I quote David Ray, who insisted that his students write poems about the little things in life and inconsequential moments—not just the big stuff. I talk with the students about the limitations that arise from a conventional view of poetry, urging them to write poems that are direct and to the point, concerned with using today's language, not the "poetic" voice of some famous generation past. The poems of David Ray, Lucille Clifton, and Edward Field (see Bibliography) provide excellent models of accessibility and contemporary voice.

To show these students how far ahead they already are, at least compared to where I was when I was seventeen, I recite the poem I wrote during my senior year of high school. They already know without my telling them, alas, that this was written many years ago, way back in the Dark Ages, when someone named Eisenhower was President.

The Tears of Separation

When at night I clamber, up the stairs and to my room,
Visions of the days gone by over me doth loom.
I picture long gone memories of a love that was so true,
But mostly, long gone darling, I envision you.

Burning tears that sting my eyes are cooled on pallid cheek,
Then fall to the pillow 'neath me, my heart is growing weak,
As I think of the woman that I loved, loved then as now I do:
Oh yes, my long gone darling, I always will love you.

It was many years ago, I yet recall the day
When the savage sea swept o'er you, taking far away,
The woman that I loved, loved then as now I do,
Alas, my long gone darling, I always will love you.

My heart beats like a tom-tom, the love pain wracks my head
But there is consolation waiting 'neath my bed.
The gun will do it quickly, and soon, my dear, I too,
My sweet, my long gone darling, will rest in peace with you.

When I visited a nearby public high school recently, the Honors

English, ninth-grade students voted 19 to 1 their preference of this poem over one of my newer efforts. So I ham up my reading of this melodramatic palaver, then select a tried-and-true poem, one that I wrote a mere five years ago. I am hoping to show the students what I mean when I suggest that, although they need not feel limited by their own experience in life, they should be using the language and themes of their own time.

The Sandman

So I was coming around the corner, and the car ahead of me has stopped and I'm on sheer ice and my car starts to skid and there's this guy on the sidewalk with a shovel and just before my car crunches into the car ahead of me he throws a shovelful of sand under my rear tires and my car comes to a stop ten feet from disaster.

Half an hour later I'm at the Xerox machine with a job I've gotta have copied in time for the mail, which leaves in ten minutes and the machine jams and I'm trying to get the paper out and something throws a spark and ignites the paper so smoke is starting to curl from the ink drum and I'm trying to figure whether I should run to the men's room for a handful of water when this guy appears with a shovel and throws a shovelful of sand into the machine's underbelly and the smoking stops.

This group is advanced enough (or my reading is sufficiently prejudicial) that the students unanimously vote their preference of the second poem. And, pleasing me enormously, they notice the influence of Edgar Allen Poe on my early poem and agree that my stuffy old Humanities teacher missed the mark when he wrote, above the title, "Out-Shelleying Shelley? C–." I had been trying to out-Poe Poe! His failure to recognize this disappointed me even more than the miserly grade. The poem certainly lacks sincerity or credibility: Is that what he meant by the reference to Shelley?

Having long ago given up on me, my teacher missed the boat. He might have asked me why the meter and rhyme seemed so heavy and demanding in my poem, and whether they were dictating the content of my words. Aside from the fancy use of language, did I have anything to say for myself? Oh well, in a week school would be over for the year.

Encouraged by their energy, if not by the intentional vagueness of their poems, I tell the students that every night they will have an open homework assignment, that is, to write a new poem each night, outside of class. They may write about anything they choose. The only stipulation is that they may not spend more than thirty minutes a night on this homework. I'm not sure why, but limiting the amount of time allowed for homework almost always ensures that each student will actually *do* it!

And this proves to be the case. But perceptive and open as they are, these students will not relent on the issue of specificity. My response to most of the poems is "I don't get it!" to which the author often responds that I wasn't supposed to! During our third meeting, I suggest a little game wherein a student reads a new poem aloud and the rest of us tell the author what we think the poem is about. The author is allowed to respond only when the audience has exhausted its interpretations and comments. The students enjoy this game, but I can see that they tire of the slow pace, a pace roughly equal to that I'd pursue in an advanced poetry workshop, where an average of fifteen minutes is given not to guessing what it is about, but to discussing the strategies of each poem, debating word choice and use of metaphor, discussing which lines might be overwritten.

Being able to *see* the poem as it is being read aloud, either in hard copy or with the use of an overhead projector, stimulates useful, reference-specific comment after the author has read the poem aloud, more than doubling the amount of productive response typically generated when students can only hear the poem. Allowing fifteen minutes for each poem works fairly well in two-hour workshops, but the timing will need to be adjusted for shorter classes. During our fourth session, realizing that the students are producing far more poems than we can discuss in any detail, I institute "read-arounds," when we can each choose to pass, as in poker, or to read a new poem, without receiving comment. We quickly discover that the read-around offers a sense of audience that is very different from that when the group listens in anticipation of offering a critique. It also provides a chance for me to read my own, new poem without using up the kind of time required when the group is expected to respond. Even with groups of thirty students or more, an occasional read-around can be worked into short class periods.

At the end of our fourth meeting, I ask the group: "What can we do to change things, maybe improve our sessions?" The response is unanimous. *It's as if they've been waiting for me to ask!* "Give us little quick-write assignments, you know, the kind you gave the first day we met."

"Why sure," I answer, and fumble back in my notebook to see that in our first session I instructed the students to "turn off their quality meter" and write as fast as they could—seven minutes nonstop—in an effort to define poetry. (The next day I suggested that each student write a poem as an example of the definition and a second poem in direct contradiction of the definition.)

Following the students' advice, to start our fifth session, I write a brief phrase on the chalkboard: *Upside Down.* We spend no more than five minutes, writing spontaneously, as fast as we can. Then we read our little poems in a read-around, without comment, from our circle of one-piece chair-desks, those unlikely contraptions within which one feels simultaneously secure and imprisoned. Here are two, written by students in this class.

Upside Down
Marian Miller

Upside down
like the grin of a depressing clown
whirling round-and-round
under a heated tent in a nameless town

Upside Down
Rose Squires

As my head rests on the carpet
The floor becomes the ceiling
It looks so clean and put together
Not like the old floor
That's the way it should be
Clutter on the ceiling
Cleanliness on the floor

I notice that our listening capacities begin to fade after the third or fourth poem, so after a brief discussion of plagiarism, I ask the students if anyone minds our "stealing" favorite lines from each other by writing them into our notebooks as we hear them. No one objects. "If you don't want to offer your lines for anyone who wants to use them, you can simply pass when your turn comes," I announce. No one passes. The students clearly enjoy reading their work aloud.

But after a day of this, they tell me that the stealing impairs their ability to listen. We change the rules: Each person will read his or her little poem *twice.* An unforeseen by-product of this is that the second reading frees many of us to experiment with a variety of reading styles.

After the last little poem has been read (now twice), we take turns, in our circle, reading to the group the lines we have stolen, reading them as if they form a unified poem. This gives each of us further opportunity to practice our reading styles, this time on material that is not our own. We are amazed to find that what one person has stolen has often been selected by others. We seem to have a common appreciation of what's worth our attention!

Each day thereafter I write a new, brief phrase: Inside Out, Left Out, A Repetitive Act (use all five senses), Plea, Reunion, The Big Game, Anniversary. I do not know what phrase I will write until I am at the board, grasping for little scenarios, ones to which I think *I* can respond!

Left Out

lost my spot in your slimy heart
that little baby in your flesh
my color dulled and not so woolly
wanting to be squashed between four breasts

I feel like a fire
the world is the burned out shell of the Garden of Eden
I heard it said that we're a herd
Accepting some ass-kissing at a pre-arranged place

a set of rules for everyone else and no one will tell me
making jokes of which I'm not a part
my steel pleasures are left out in the rain
lunch hasn't settled

no one alone no one ugly like me
only the refrigerator is my ally
laughter that has no meaning
just moving on one leg is the biggest pain of all

dirt crawls off the back of your shoes
all the way to whipdedoo first base
laughing to the echo of myself

These are the lines I have listed in my notebook from the small-poem read-around for "Left Out." Doing my homework, which is to make the stolen lines into a finished poem, I come up with the following revision.

My slimy heart, that throbbing baby,
couldn't grasp love before it dulled
like the burned-out shell of the Garden of Eden.
I heard it said that we're a herd of rules for everyone else
That no one will tell me:
jokes of which I'm no longer a part,
a toy left in the rain
all fall to rust.

I ask the students whether they think *fall* in the final line is a verb or a noun, meaning "everything *falls* to rust" or "the toy is in the rain all *fall,*" September till December. With a different group of students, this ambiguity might set off a prolonged discussion, but this group wants to *write poems*. These students don't much care for discussing theory!

These exercises give each writer a sense of his or her most memorable lines while underscoring the importance of *the line* as the building block of poetry. The students are still writing independently, love and death poems of numbing abstraction to which we now give the second hour of our daily session, but they are also creating little five-minute wonders, on demand, in class. And one or two of the students are already coming to see that the "throwaway poems" we're creating spontaneously with little or no inspiration other than an arbitrary title, are usually better understood than their labored homework efforts in the name of poetry.

"I like these assignments better than those where we have little room for interpretation," says Shannon. "'The Big Game,' for instance, is different for each of us."

As Linda Rief says in *Seeking Diversity:* "When I have a question, I always ask the kids, and we figure out a solution together. I have faith in my students that they know best what works for them and what they are capable of doing" (1992, 185). What I like best about teaching is that my little theories are constantly challenged. Until working with this group, I did not believe that good poems could be produced on demand. Or is it that when students see their recommendations taken seriously, they become invested in making the class work?

Exercises

If good poems are rarely written on demand, isn't it quixotic to ask students to write poems in response to specific assignments? In most job and academic environments, people are occasionally asked to write on demand. But rarely, if ever, are they asked to write *poetry* on demand. Yet writing poems fosters an appreciation for language and builds skills that enhance all other forms of writing. This suggests that, in every academic discipline, writing poems and other forms of linguistic play should be an integral part of the curriculum!

Here are a few ideas that may help loosen up a writing group, perhaps help create an atmosphere that encourages experimentation.

1. Turn off your quality meter and write a seven-minute definition of poetry.
2. Now write a poem that exemplifies your definition of poetry.
3. Now write one that demonstrates properties that are opposite to those in the poem you defined.
4. What kinds of language use do you overhear in everyday conversation? Take commonly used phrases, or a specific conversation, and build a short poem.
5. What is the role of awkward or naïve use of language? Find unique phrases or expressions in an infant's, adult's, or your own speech patterns, and build them into a poem.
6. Write an old-fashioned, melodramatic poem, composed of rhymed, metered quatrains.

INSIDE OUT

INSIDE I FEEL ALL WARM
LIKE ONE OF THOSE
KOSHY COFFEE DRINKS;
MY STONE BONES CRAWL
WITHIN THE VERY CENTER OF
MY BODY,
AND BEFORE I CHOOSE TO STOP
I SIGH,
A WARMISH HEAVE

THIS IS INSIDE
COMING
OUT

▼

This poem is a nice combination of simplicity and word choice. The poem is very basic, although the subject could be elaborated upon. I do not believe that "koshy" is actually a word, although the sound of it brings about a nice warm feeling. This adds to the intent of the poem. The ending ties in with the title of the poem.

—*Claire Feldman*

2
Experiments
persona, discovery, and reflection

Poetry is a place where the mind and heart can play with information, a place where anything goes, a place where we may or may not be attempting to create "art," and where we are constantly experimenting. As such, it also offers a comfortable means for reflection on the lessons we have learned!

Exposure to forms and the challenge to write in a variety of poetic forms are essential, but a repetitive, year after year academic focus on only one or two of the best-known forms (especially acrostics, pantoum, and rhymed, metrical quatrains) gives poetry writing a bad name.

Good writers experiment with form, testing their skills, experiencing the power that can be wrung from words constrained in some dimension. But many teenage writers do not yet have the patience for long deliberations over multiple drafts (of poems), so the goal of a poetry class might be to have students develop an *awareness* (not mastery) of ten or twelve major forms, writing ten or twelve poems, at least one in each of the forms.

Another approach is to encourage students to invent their own poetic forms. A motivated student might write a 47-line free-verse poem, then describe its technical properties, albeit derived arbitrarily, as the "rules" for that genre of poem. For all we know, this is how musician Dennis Murphy invented "Doo-dah," which he defines as "a work of art in which two things with no apparent connection are featured." Murphy has written an impressive number of Doo-dah poems, "which tend to be short," he says. He has also created several Doo-dah paintings. "I suppose the Doo-dah Movement is a branch of surrealism, or a less iconoclastic form of Dada," he muses.

At early grades, students may feel compelled to parrot nursery rhymes in established modes. It's only a small jump from imitation to effective, even touching work, such as this poem by a student at North Bennington (Vermont) Elementary School.

Untitled
James Reynolds

I wish I was a wish upon a star.
I wish I was a wish upon my heart.

Teenage and adult poets often create their work around slightly more complex structures, such as "The Night Before Christmas," or some other poem that establishes a productive cadence in the mind of the composer.

I love to acknowledge such accomplishments, listening for moments of humor, enjoying the sounds and rhythms, the roots of spoken communication, the play! But I want to remember that, starting in the primary grades, and certainly by the time they reach high school, students are ready to write completely original poems, poems that establish their own cadences, their own rhyme schemes, their own unique forms.

Even in elementary school, young writers deserve exposure to poetry as a tool for serious exploration and communication, not just a vehicle for amusing the reader. And, for all the emphasis a poetry curriculum might place on specific forms, whether nursery rhyme or epic, I propose a parallel curriculum that provides a rich background in poetry as free verse! Here, for example, is a dead-serious poem by a dead-serious author, David Ray, that fourth-grade students (and adults alike) might enjoy discussing.

Fourth of July

My uncle,
Great Norman,
Whose leg was full of
Finest German steel,
Broke three chairs and a table
When the kids
Set off firecrackers
On July 4, 1946,
Just after apple pie.

This poem is remarkable for how much information it contains and what that information suggests. A single sentence, it might nevertheless be accepted as an outline for a novel. At least that's what I claim, preparing for a discussion of how we define *novel*, and making ready to justify the hyperbole of my claim that such a short poem *may even be* a novel!

I try not to prolong any discussion of technical matters because I believe that, as in teaching grammar, it's only when the students are hooked on *the content* that they'll start to care about the technicalities. Infants learn to speak by imitating the sounds of their elders; in similar fashion, we can teach poem writing by presenting our students with clear models, encouraging imitation or parody. A young author might use the voice of one poem to address the subject of another, while, on a parallel track, writing poems that establish their own, unique voice and subjects for poetic expression.

Poetry and the Other Arts

Considering poetry's relationship to the other art forms helps students bring to their poetry some of the principles they may have learned—perhaps without ever articulating them—from their work in other artistic disciplines. It is perfectly possible for five-year-olds to beat a drum or for executives to tap their fingers in rhythmic fashion without understanding that they are repeating patterns that establish a rhythm. It is equally possible for a person to paint a landscape without thinking about the contribution that contrast is making to the quality of the painting. Pointing out such components to the creator often encourages that person to try future experiments with each of them, together and in isolation.

What is poetry's relationship to prose writing? How is poetry different? This is another way to work toward useful definitions of *poetry*, even though the answers may, at times, contradict each other. A poem may be a short verbal burst of feeling, expressed entirely in phrases or in flashes of imagery. On the other hand, like prose fiction, a poem may unveil a plot, complete with setting, character, dialogue, and a variety of emotions.

What is poetry's relationship to music? Well, it is often combined with music to make songs, from rap to romantic waltzes. Poetry often has a specific rhythm, as does most music. Some poems seem to exist without any form of accompaniment, not even an identifiable rhythm, just as some music is performed without words or rhythmic pattern.

What about painting? Painters rely on *contrast;* without contrast their images would be invisible. Poems often rely on contrast for their effect. Painters also speak of rhythm and tone, major components of poetry. An image or color recurring throughout a painting may provide a sense of rhythm, or perhaps a painter mentions rhythm in reference to moving a brush across the surface. Tone can refer to how the painting strikes the viewer: Is it dark? unhappy? jazzy? silly? exuberant? Paintings also work with shape, just like a poem on the page!

How about dance? Modern dance is to theatre what poetry is to the novel. With few exceptions dance and poetry are briefer than their proscenium and prose counterparts. But also, modern dance does not usually rely on language or the conventions of theatre to get its point across. Poetry, too, often takes liberties that cannot be sustained in a conventional novel.

What is poetry's relationship to theatre? Theatre almost always investigates human character; poetry may do the same. Theatre almost always has a setting; poetry can have a specific setting, too. Theatre usually has a plot, with a climax; poetry has that option. Affected by a director's choices, theatre uses color, pace, rhythm, contrast, tone, vocal expression, physical attitude and placement of the actors. Poetry has its equivalents to all these components.

Learning Styles and Multiple Intelligences

For all my years of working in the classroom, I only recently paid serious attention to learning styles and multiple intelligences. After all, I reasoned, poetry writing *invites* the author to investigate or reveal specific styles and intelligences, because poems are verbal or graphic or musical or kinetic or ... by nature.

What I hadn't considered, however, was that the assignments I made were almost uniformly oral. A great advantage of this was that it invited a panoply of interpretations. Yes, I would write on the board to show a rhyme scheme or a form, but when I made the actual assignment, I'd simply rattle it off orally, responding to all questions by saying, "The answer is whatever you want it to be."

But some students are initially confused by this approach and now I recognize that they need time to develop trust in themselves *and in me* before they can let go, and risk doing the assignment "wrong." And one of the best ways to help each student find the place of letting go is to pitch the assignment toward a variety of learning styles. Recognizing four learning styles, for instance, means pitching each assignment in four ways:

1. Here's the definition of a sonnet (verbal);

2. Here's an example of a sonnet (concrete);

3. In groups of three, each group write a quatrain (collaborative);

4. One member of each group volunteers to read the group's quatrain while the other two members dance or mime, or a volunteer improvises dance or mime as the others translate actions into words (verbal/kinetic).

Find ways to lift off the page what your students are writing. Is there a theatre group of four or five students who'd like to create staged interpretations of a poem? Do some painters want to illustrate poems or create sets for the theatre project? How about setting some of these poems to music? And choreographers: Can some of these poems be danced?

Several years ago, I was writing teacher at a weeklong summer arts conference on Star Island, off the coast of Portsmouth, New Hampshire. One afternoon the oil-painting teacher and I merged her students with the writers in my workshop. We had the writers create stories and poems from the painters' work, while the painters made visual art from the writers' work. These were brief—half-hour—studies. Then the painters and the writers swapped their new paintings and writings for the work of a writer or painter who was new to them. In this way, we completed a round in the game of "Telephone." An original painting was shown, followed by its verbal translation by a different person, followed by the latest visual rendering by yet another person, who based it on the verbal translation. Comparing the original painting to the second painting, and comparing written passages that were linked only by a painting, provided plenty of laughs and who knows what bits of individual learning?

Using these types of collaborative, interarts exercises, students can form temporary production units, collaborating on the creation of new, interdisciplinary work. But, as with any endeavor that relies on bringing two classrooms together for a collaborative project, careful planning is essential!

And, as any experienced teacher will verify, thoughtful reflection on the activity, a few hours or days after the fact, will lead to an even better experience in the future.

A Little Case Study of a Little Failure

This kind of interdisciplinary experimentation is essential to my excitement in the classroom. If I am merely repeating activities that have worked for me previously, I lose interest and the students, somehow, can sense my lack of enthusiasm. So it's important for me always to be experimenting and reflecting on the results. Recently, I was asked to design an interdisciplinary collaboration among middle school student photographers and elementary writers in Waits River, Vermont, where I met, among other lively students, a young girl named Alicia.

Alicia is the kind of fourth-grade girl one sees in Disney movies. Beneath her bangs and behind her dark-framed glasses (over which she comically peers, schoolmarm style), deep-set eyes usually reflect merriment and intensity.

So when I saw the look on Alicia's face, as she quietly fought tears, I realized the failure of my project. As the fourth through eighth grade "writer in residence," I had promised, during two of my seven visits, to link my fourth-grade writing students with the eighth-grade, first-time photographers who were being taught by another artist-in-residence. I explained to the younger students that they would act as "directors," telling the older students what to photograph and how.

In preparation for the special class when she would have a photographer at her disposal, Alicia brought her stuffed toy penguin to school for a series of portraits in the playground's snow. She had believed me when I told each student, "A week after directing a 'photo shoot,' each of you will receive a photograph or two that you have planned, a photograph you may want to amplify with a poem."

The penguin shots never turned up in the large envelopes of black-and-white prints that were delivered a week later. Not only Alicia, but many of my other young writers were disappointed by what came back, as I apologized for glitches that had surely been foreseeable. "You can just work with a different photograph," I said to student after unhappy student, amassing a slush pile of rejected photographs from which they could choose.

My vision of the project had not materialized, but especially for those students who found (or witnessed another's) satisfaction in translating disappointing or irrelevant photographs into words, the experience carried important lessons.

- The worst raw material sometimes makes the best art.
- Take what you're given, what surrounds you, and *use it!*
- The communication of focus to a second party, who must then communicate to a machine, is tricky.

Given that the two days scheduled for this project taught these valuable lessons, the failure to realize my vision is incidental. Yet if I had it to do over, I'd prepare the students to expect, at the least, a "shift of vision" upon delivery of the photographs. I might also carry to class a cache of photographic postcards to supplement the slush pile, keeping their existence a secret, offered only in dire, individual circumstances. And I would completely rethink the presumption that elementary-level students would not be intimidated by the reversal of roles they would face in their forty-five minutes with an older student.

The day after Alicia's disappointment, her characteristic ebullience returned as she read a poem she'd written about a photograph from the slush pile. And I was ready, once again, to try something new with a bunch of unsuspecting young people!

Exercises

1. Take an existing nursery rhyme and, using its meter and rhyme, write a poem that establishes a completely different mood.

2. Write a poem that compares the habits of a wild animal to one of your personal habits.

3. Create a short poem that puts an event into historic context.

4. Write a letter from the point of view of someone who is far away, either fighting a war, spying, or exploring remote parts of the world. The letter is being written to either a lover, a parent, or a whole family back home. What *scenes* can the letter communicate? What kind of language does the writer use? What does this tell us about the writer? Make the letter look authentic—a relic. If it's written by someone who is in the wilderness or high on an icy mountain, maybe it is all folded and has water stains! How's the writer's spelling? What questions does the writer ask in this letter? Are they in a consecutive list?

5. Rewrite the letter as a telegram where every word costs one dollar to send. What are the most important details?

6. Go back to the letter and the telegram and look for phrases that would work as the basis for an entire poem.

After Dinner

I see myself in the mirror
I am half a reflection
half a man,
I admit that I have
your lipstick,
that dark burgundy color
you used to wear
whenever
we went out,
and
to remember you
more vividly
I smear it
on
my own lips
regularly
after dinner

▼

Here I was able to take a freewrite that I was not very fond of and revise one line into an entire poem. The poem simply depicts an outlandish situation that cries out to the reader as such extreme desperation that it becomes humorous. There are no intended hidden meanings, the poem is completely straightforward.

I believe that of all my poems, this poem has gone through the most revisions. I continuously shaved off unnecessary words to obtain the effect of blunt humor. This process was similar to that of writing a news article.

I had the most fun pretending that I was male, which is something I rarely do in persona poems. However, the gender added to the humor. People find it easier to laugh at males who are desperate than at females. Actually, I believe that people in our society find it easier to laugh at males, period. For example, if the narrator of the poem were a woman who used her ex's cologne after dinner, the effect would not be the same.

—*Claire Feldman*

3

Finding Topics, Providing Attitude, and Guiding Revision

Unplanned Collaboration

Even the best writing assignments grow stale. The first time, with almost any writing assignment for which I feel excitement, students (and I) respond well. The writing is fresh, the ideas and images are new. Remembering such assignments, which often arise spontaneously in response to what's already going on in the classroom, I sometimes try them again with a new group of students. It's almost like telling a joke: Even with a fresh audience each time, the more times I tell it, the less laughter it provokes.

But one writing assignment never fails me; I use it as the opening exercise with almost any group of writers, regardless of age. In just seven minutes, each participant contributes to, and then becomes owner of a rough draft—a healthy clump of words and images—from which to fashion a poem. But I never reveal that I think the product of this effort will be the first draft of a collaborative poem.

After explaining that my method of writing is to write as fast as possible, ignoring concerns for quality and accuracy during the process of composition, I abruptly introduce the dreaded moment: "Take out a pencil and a piece of paper."

I am about to ask each person in the room to write a simple phrase. Regardless of the sophistication of the participants, I review the definition of a *phrase*. Then, as quickly as possible, the instructions are delivered: "Write a phrase—not a complete sentence, just a phrase—for some observation you experienced between waking this morning and arriving at this workshop. You have twenty-two seconds. Pencils up, get set . . . Write!"

It's important that, at the moment I call out "Write!" I apply my own pencil to the page, scrawling out whatever phrase I can. Then, at random, I call on the participants to read their phrases, making sure they don't "tell" what they've written, but read directly from the page. (More often than not, the "told" version varies from what has been written, sometimes mushier, less direct, than what is actually on the page.)

On newsprint or a chalkboard, I write each phrase on its own line and ask the participants to enter the same lines in their notebooks. Somewhere in the process I add my own phrase, and continue seeking offerings until everyone has contributed or until I've used up the space on my newsprint or chalkboard, whichever comes first. A lot of sonnets are born this way!

As I take dictation, I model my own, homemade form of shorthand, trying to keep up with each offering. Here is the response a group of high school students generated, shorthand translated back into full words:

> There are a lot more stoplights on Route 15 than there were in 1968
> House with a pond!
> Sadie on top of the gravel pile
> Damp blank closed sky
> Rilla running around the room, "I'm naked Daddy!"
> Beautiful mother and daughter.
> A small bird sweeping toward my windshield.
> A squirrel works an apple back up a tree.
> Distance where I least expected it
> Showerhead sprays in a circle
> Fog—hanging on hillsides
> "Bove and Fagan" on the ice cream truck
> Everybody up down

I write exactly what the participants dictate, asking about punctuation, the spelling of homonyms (often an opportunity for laughter and a lesson on wordplay), and being sure each writer reads directly from the page. Then I read the responses aloud, carefully and slowly, using my voice to smooth over the rough spots, running the end of one phrase into the beginning of another ("enjambment") to create unforeseen sentences. I present the piece as if it were the well-polished final draft of a master. "Okay, what do we have here?" I ask.

Students will often respond, "A poem!"

"All right, maybe so. But what makes it a poem?"

"It's all about the same thing—you know, morning images."

"Plus, the way you read it made it sound like a poem."

I make sure to mention that, indeed, almost any piece of writing can be made to sound pretty good if it's read well. The reader's attention to speaking skills enhances the audience's response to a piece of writing. Even a diverse listing of images and phrases from different students—the equivalent of a bunch of random impulses from the individual writer's brain—can usually be made to sound like a unified piece. "Read your work with assurance and pride," I say, "and you can sell cowflops for apple pies!" It might be argued that reading aloud becomes, in fact, a revision of the piece.

"Be sure you have copied these lines into your notebooks. I'm going to ask you to use this as your first draft and, for homework, to revise it into a poem that you've changed so much you can call it your own. Here are ways I might consider revising the piece. . . ." Spontaneously, now, I want to show as many strategies for revision as I can, announcing my biases as I go.

I give my revision a title.

Return

A lot more stoplights now on route 15 [**cut dead language**]
Than in 1968, but there's still that house with the pond!
And Sadie still sits on top of the gravel pile
In damp, blank, closed sky. [**add filler words to create continuity**]

Inside that house I know Rilla runs around the room:
"I'm naked, Daddy!" Beautiful mother and daughter,
Small birds swoop my windshield [**revise participles into *real* verbs, verbs with *tense!*]**
While a squirrel works an apple back up the tree.

Distance where I least expected it, once my home
I've got a motel where the showerhead sprays in a circle: [**add "once my home/ I've got a motel" for continuity; keep the strong image of the showerhead**]
My window looks out on hillside fog
And a Bove and Fagan ice cream truck
As music plays.

"Needless to say, this was a fast, almost thoughtless revision, just to show the kinds of changes you might want to consider. When I do my homework, I'll review these revisions, reconsidering each one. Revision often leads to improvement, but it doesn't always make things better!"

I invited writing teacher and author Barry Lane to write his own revision on the basis of the original text.

Red Light 10 A.M. June 17, 1991

A small bird swoops
toward my windshield
Sadie at the top of
the gravel pile,
Damp
Blank
Closed
sky.
I think of
Rilla running
around the room,
last night,
"I'm naked Daddy!"
"I'm naked Daddy!"

Beautiful mother
    and daughter
this morning
at the breakfast table
eating
milk soaked
Cheerios

Outside,
A squirrel works an
    apple back
    up the tree.

Distance,
where I least
expected it.
Showerhead sprays
in a circle,
Fog hangs on
hillsides

More stoplights
on route 15
than there were in
1968

I recommend that this exercise be initiated without a hint that the product may turn out to be a poem because, all too often, when students think of poetry, they conjure archaic romanticisms instead of immediate imagery, "truth is beauty" vs. the squirrel with the apple.

In their revisions, some students will use only one or two lines of the original poem as a starting point or a central image. No matter how these revisions are accomplished, I try to remember to provide an opportunity for participants to read and discuss their final-draft responses, although I'm equally intent on moving on to something new.

What's important to me, in this assignment, is that students develop a broader awareness of poetic strategies, of the benefits of speaking distinctly and with feeling, and of a variety of approaches to revision. Maybe because this exercise covers all three of those bases and because it is group-oriented and fast, it is the only one in my little satchel of tricks that never seems to fail.

Finding Topics

Finding topics is the easy part. You can always blindfold someone and have that person pin the tail on an open dictionary. The one time I tried this, I got *oomphora*. Ever since, I've been able to come up with topics unassisted! Central to any topic is *attitude* or *circumstance*. Either, of itself, provides cause for a poem as well as a topic can, and often provides the best starting place for a poem. Adding the writer's point of view to these variables will create a dynamic situation that, of itself, should impel the hand to scribble. A topic can emerge from attitude, from the writer's choice of circumstances, or the selected point of view.

- *Attitude:* anger or syrupy sarcasm or utter joy
- *Circumstance:* a wedding or a funeral or a graduation or a prom
- *Point of view* (examples here are provided only for a wedding): A bridesmaid, or younger sister or brother of the bride or groom, or an usher, or a parent of the bride or groom, or a former sweetheart of the bride or groom, or the church official performing the ceremony
- *Topic:* being left behind or preparing the floral arrangements or greeting the guests or thinking private thoughts about whether the bride and groom will make a "good couple"

All of these components should be brainstormed with the class, so that a variety of possibilities is listed.

Think about the different learning styles: Some students may best come up with poems by first acting or dancing them, allowing language to surface at the same time or after its kinetic expression! David Schein, a playwright and actor, tells me that his face takes on the physical expressions of the character for whom he is writing dialogue. For the moment, he looks and talks just like the character: He *is* the character. His face gets quite a workout when he writes rapid-fire verbal exchanges.

When helping students find something to write about, it's also a good idea to offer choices, and to allow, as a topic, "anything else you want." This frees many reluctant students, and takes the pressure off anyone who may not want to write in response to whatever the day's writing challenges happen to be. People learn to write by writing, not by wondering what to write about or how to approach the topic, so what is important to me is only that each student actually *write*, not chew on the end of the implement, . . . thinking . . ., a writer's worst habit.

Form is another tumbler in the lock that may need a turn. Suggesting a form often helps a writer find words, just as playing background music sometimes helps poets find rhythm. Imposing a form may be the equivalent of telling students they may not spend more than half an hour on their homework: It defines the task.

Repetition is another possibility. The simple repeating of a structure or image establishes a rhythm (both aural and visual) that quickly transmits poetic intent. The following poem by student Ryan Harris, "When the Circles Have the Remote Control the Triangles Don't Get the Point," was written as part of a theatre and poetry improvisation class that David Schein and I co-taught at the Governor's Institute on the Arts. Notice the nearly hypnotic effect the poem creates visually *and* when read aloud.

> When I have the remote control I watch my favorite sunset over
>   and over . . .
> When you have the remote control you remember what it was like
>   to be a senior citizen
> When he has the remote control he finds a way
> When we have the remote control we allow something to come
>   between us
> When you have the remote control you steal my heart
> When they have the remote control they play our games and take
>   our credit
> When Grandma has the remote control she makes Sunday dinners
>   that last two weeks
> When Dad has the remote control he forgets that money isn't
>   everything

When the winter has the remote control the oil company is very
    happy
When anger has the remote control this might be the last thing you
    ever hear
When joy had the remote control I wrote that story that Molly read
    yesterday.
When greed has the remote control you are not your own
When Geof had the remote control I wrote this poem
stop pause click rewind
playing with the contrast, balance, time
change when the grass was still green wasn't it
When we have the remote control we give it up
When the remote has us we have lost

Add to form a category called *variables*, and one can revisit the essential components of English, a review that is essential with *any* group of student poets, regardless of age. Teaching all grades, including adults who are returning, midcareer, to college, I am continually reminded that my knowing the difference between first and second person, for instance, doesn't mean that anyone else in the room has any idea what I'm talking about.

Writers often apply person to their work unconsciously. Same with tense. This is fine, even desirable, because it implies an unselfconscious flow of language. But when the writer revisits that "unselfconscious flow" with revision in mind, a keen awareness of person and tense is indispensable.

Take a look at "The Sandman," in Chapter 1. What would happen if the narrator unified the tense in the opening lines, instead of jumping from the past ("So I *was coming* around the corner") to the present ("and the car ahead of me *has stopped* and *I'm* on sheer ice and my car *starts to skid . . .*")? And what would be the effect if the entire first paragraph, presented as one run-on sentence, were broken into more manageable units? What if the second paragraph, also a single, run-on sentence, received the same treatment? If these changes were made, the piece would be more grammatical, but would it lose its spontaneity?

What if the piece were written completely in the past tense? Would some of the excitement, some of the narrator's frustration, melt away? What about the narrative voice we use when we orally recount an experience or tell a joke? How carefully do we, in informal speech, unify tense? "So I was coming down the stairs for breakfast and I smell bacon and eggs frying in a lot of lard, which means my father was at the stove."

I start to talk about the first person, present tense, and everyone in the room begins to nod, knowingly. There's something about all this nodding I

AN IDEA WHEEL

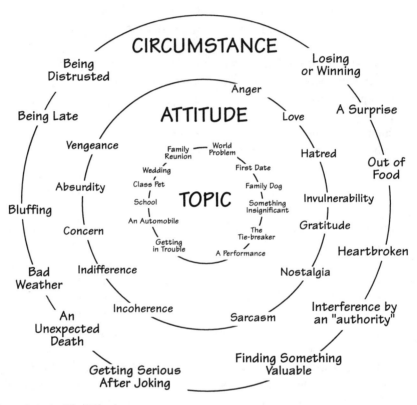

Figure 3–1. *An Idea Wheel*

don't quite trust. "Okay, who can give me an example of a sentence that's in the first person?" I must never forget that the vocabulary I'm so casually throwing around may well be complete gibberish to some of my students, no matter their age or educational background!

Remembering that my goal is only to have students write two or three poems a week, and to enjoy the process, I never take the assignments I make too seriously. Writing poetry is not so much a matter of following directions as it is of *using* the directions, or independently *finding* direction. The assignment, after all, is only a prompt intended to help the students focus their verbal energy. They are equally helped when they see that I am much less interested in whether they fulfilled all my specifications than I am in the results of their experimenting.

Having said that, I want to explain the idea wheel, a simple tool for helping everyone find a unique writing assignment. The key is the writer's willingness to accept, for a poem's starting point, the combination of topic, attitude, and circumstance that comes up when the wheel is spun!

Twelve specific descriptions can each serve as one of twelve points on each wheel. So, for *Topic*, one might enter: A wedding; Family reunion; School; First date; The tie-breaker; A performance; Getting in trouble; Class pet; Family dog; An automobile; World problem; Something insignificant. Upon the *Attitude* wheel, one might enter: Anger; Gratitude; Love; Hatred; Sarcasm; Invulnerability; Nostalgia; Incoherence; Indifference; Concern; Absurdity; Vengeance. If one were working with only a *Topic* and an *Attitude* wheel, the twelve ideas on each list would yield (12 x 12) 144 possible combinations! 1728 combinations are possible by adding a *Circumstance* wheel, which might list: Bad weather; Being late; Heartbroken; A surprise; Bluffing; Getting serious after some joking; Interference by an "authority"; Being distrusted; Losing or winning; Out of food; An unexpected death; Finding something valuable. Needless to say, by adding larger, outer wheels, one enormously enlarges the number of possibilities. A series of clock faces might be used, with the numbers keyed to a chart that presents the corresponding attitudes, circumstances, and so forth. Students can spin these wheels to find helpful suggestions. Or, using poems by their peers, students can find listings for their own idea wheels. From the following poem "All in the Course of Time," by Denis Lambert, a student, one might lift, for *Topic* alone, Time, Ocean, Forests, Environment, Growth, Change, Life, Death, Epidemic, Nourishment, Relationship, and Dreams.

> What happens to those who sit still as time passes?
> The sky is blue, but the ocean has changed color.
> The grass is green, but the forests are disappearing.
> The sun is orange, but people suffer.
>
> What are you doing?
>
> Growth, change, life, death
> But still the sky is blue, the grass: green, the sun:
> orange.
>
> What are you doing?
>
> Like the rising and the falling of the sun
> Epidemics come and go
> In the course of
> One year

What are you doing?

Unappreciated, unnurtured, and undernourished
Plants lose their leaves
In the course of
      One month

What are you doing?

Long, meaningful, loving relationships
Self-destruct and break
In the course of
      One week

Growth, change, life, death
What are you doing?

Last word spoken and last breath taken
Beings move on to another world
In only
      A moment

Hopes become realities
And dreams come true
We have
      but
         a
            lifetime.

Focused Revision

Few writers work entirely in their heads, polishing each line before they write. For most of us, it's important to *see* the words and to make changes in the text of the poem by crossing out, drawing arrows, and otherwise marking it up. Students need to witness this process, so—as described earlier in this chapter—I almost always try a quick, spontaneous, public revision on the board at the start of a semester. I also provide examples of revision by deletion and revision by expansion. Students are often astounded to see how dramatic revisions can be, amazed to see that some writers toss out, wholesale, so much of their work. I remind them of the ratios of raw footage to edited film that are reported by commercial filmmakers: twenty-to-one is typical. Yet many writers, even though words are much easier to come by than film stock, are reluctant to abandon such a large percentage of their first-draft work.

Revision doesn't always make it better. Sometimes the spontaneous expression of a line is lost when the author works on it too much. So I insist that students keep copies of each draft of their work, hard copy in the case of students who use computers.

But revision serves purposes beyond improving the poem. Through the act of revision a writer acquires information and skills that will inform *future* work. It is through revision, most often, that an author finds opportunity to experiment with the effect of breaking lines in a syllabic pattern, to play with the shape of the poem, to delete lines or whole stanzas, to shift focus or mood, to introduce factual information, to delete or add an expression of feeling.

Because students have often used revision simply to edit and recopy their work, they are often intrigued to see, briefly, examples of work in progress where dramatic changes have resulted from a few strokes of the pen. The following example, from my notebook, shows how much a poem can gain from revision by deletion.

Memory (first draft)

When I was in 6th grade
I chipped a tooth
when I tried to chew through a wire
instead of using a wire cutter.
My parents scolded me
for being such a fool.
"You'll live with that mistake all your life,"
my father said.
Yet that tooth has always been useful,
always with me,
a built-in pair of scissors.

Edge (retitled, final draft)

The tooth that I broke,
using it instead of a knife,
now has an edge
more useful than a knife.

Some students resist the call of revision, even after I've successfully proven to their peers that revision matters . . . a lot! One of the best reasons to make quick-write assignments, allowing no more than five to seven minutes for students to respond to a poetry prompt, is to be able to point out to the reluctant reviser that since only five to seven minutes were given to the first draft, there must be some thought-through considerations that will lead to a poem's improvement.

Revision can be steered by following any of the arbitrary listings that might appear as an outside ring of variables on an idea wheel. Revise this piece by reducing all the sentences to phrases; break the piece into stanzas of five lines each, twelve syllables per line. Take one image or line from the poem and use it as the starting point for an entirely new poem or song. Reduce the piece to a telegram, now write that telegram as a haiku. Turn all the participles and gerunds into active verbs in the past tense; delete half the adjectives, replacing them with metaphors or similes. Students can brainstorm a list of ways a poem might be revised, then draw suggestions from a hat.

Each of these suggestions might be used, in turn, throughout a twelve-week course. Focused revision is the equivalent of a topic assignment or writing prompt: It makes specific what the writer can do that might improve the poem and that will provide a new way of seeing that poem. It sometimes happens that revising leads to a whole new poem, so the writer is left with *two* finished works! In one of his writing courses at the University of Vermont, author Toby Fulwiler asks his students to write several revisions, week after week, insisting that each revision be completely different from the drafts that preceded it.

Parts of Speech Revision

Parts of speech revision requires that the writer first underline all verbs, then one by one review those verbs, considering synonyms that might carry more power, or better sustain a mood, or rhythmically improve the poem. By the time they reach high school, students should know being verbs from active verbs, but they may need repeated reminders to avoid overuse of the former; they should also develop built-in "passive voice detectors," and edit their work to ensure that any use of the passive voice is intentional.

Next, the author double underlines and considers each of the adverbs, whose impact will surely have been altered if they've been modifying any of the verbs that have been changed. Adverbs used to modify adjectives or other adverbs should also be carefully evaluated. Nouns are next. I like to circle them, as well as all gerunds, and then to put rectangles around all adjectives, including the participles. If I sharpen the nouns they modify, how many adjectives can I dump? Triangles imprison the prepositions as the author considers ways to rephrase that will reduce and clarify. What's left? Articles and conjunctions. No need to mark these since they are all that is not marked. I look at each unmarked word in the poem and consider the alternatives I have.

This whole process can be endlessly recursive, for once a noun is changed the adjective may be deleted or changed, and once that has happened, the author may want to reconsider the noun again. Strengthening verb choice certainly helps to eliminate some of the adverbs, but do these excisions adversely affect the rhythm of the line? If so, can multisyllabic nouns be brought in, or can one borrow some words from the following or preceding line, or does a modifier need to be reinstated? Some nouns gain a syllable when they are plural (*rose/roses, child/children*); are there nouns that, made plural, lose a syllable? Likewise, the syllabic count of some verbs is affected by the choice of first, second, and third person (*I/you change, she changes*), and the choice of tense (*she changes/she changed, she corrects/she corrected*).

Writers who care about their best work can usually explain the alternatives they've considered for each word or phrase in a poem. They're able to explain the narrator's attitude and its relationship to word choice. And, I want to argue, they have a plausible explanation of what the poem means!

Exercises

Here are suggestions for students who may feel stuck in their approach to revision:

1. Review with an eye toward eliminating as many participles, adjectives, and adverbs as possible, strengthening as necessary the nouns and verbs they modify.

2. Counting syllables in each line, create a "syllabic poem," where each line has the same number of syllables, or where a syllabic pattern is established.

3. Rewrite the piece as if it were being told from the point of view and with the speech patterns of someone who is different from its current narrator: the Queen of England, a supermarket checkout person, a five-year-old boy, a ghost, a teacher who should have retired ten years ago.

4. Review the piece and determine whether the imagery is primarily visual, tactile, aural, olfactory, or cerebral. Create a second draft that makes use of *all* the senses or especially evokes one.

5. Take one image from the poem and use it as the first line of a new poem.

6. Look through your poems for examples of abstract language. Make a list of the abstractions in your poems, then find concrete nouns that might replace some of these abstractions in new poems.

Ad Vert Tis Ment

I am available,
a motor vehicle,
to be bought,
sold,
gift given,
I suggest you cast
a ring
as
soon
as
possible
as
you reserve me.
I will not be under bargained for,
driven downtown
in the rain,
or repaired by a sleazy man
lacking experience
because
lifting up my hood
with your own bare hands
is half the
fun!

▼

This poem began as a found poem and was revised. The strength here is the personal poem of the narrator being an object with emotions similar to those of a person. This is an experimental poem, the theme is quite clear, though the other aspect of word choice and format were more or less random. It is that sense of randomness that identifies the humor and silly content. The poem is not meant to be deep, only an experiment.

I do not feel finished with this poem. I like to entertain the idea of objects acting as human, though it is not a subject that I feel passionate about. I'm not sure how else this subject could be attacked except from a silly, juvenile angle. Overall I do not think that this poem is very strong.

—*Claire Feldman*

4

Word-machines

Writing the Shorter Forms

The Fulcrum

In their long-revered *How Does a Poem Mean?* poets John Ciardi and Miller Williams describe the *fulcrum* of a poem as a turning point, just as *fulcrum*, in physics, defines the point of optimum leverage. "Such a point of balance (and silence) may be called a *fulcrum*. . . . In briefest form, *a poem is one part against another across a silence*. To understand this characteristic of the poem is to understand the theory of poetic form. To be able to respond to it in a poem is to understand the practice of poetry" (1975, 360).

After a comprehensive discussion of the fulcrum, perhaps guarding against the overanalysis of poetry, Ciardi and Williams add a telling comment. "Any method of analysis is designed only to assure one that he is giving his human attention to the poem itself rather than to some nonpoetic paraphrase of its unenacted meaning. In every good poem there is some final echo of nuance and feeling that lies beyond explanation and analysis" (1975, 368).

At its simplest, the fulcrum might simply provide the break in a text between which two seemingly unlike objects are compared. It can also be seen as the moment when a comedian stops joking, and talks about something serious. It can be represented by a sudden shift of style; it might affect the shape of the poem or how it is performed. According to Ciardi and Williams, the fulcrum may even occur off the page, perhaps existing as the unspoken moral or point of the poem. In that a good poem uses a fulcrum and other physical principles, it might be thought of as a "word-machine."

Show students the fulcrums of existing poems and they quickly understand a basic principle of writing, often creating poems that go beyond mere description to emotional significance. Even the shortest of poems can have a fulcrum, possibly between the title and the first line of a one-line poem. Here is one I wrote after a disappointing attempt to reach a barbershop.

Hitchhiking for a Haircut Into Harrisburg, PA

My hair is still long.

Some teachers use a *double prompt* to help their students write poems with a strong fulcrum. These include:

I used to _____, but now I _____.

There once was _____; there now is _____.

This _____ used to be _____. It now is _____.

You once were _____. You now are _____.

This format ensures a compare and contrast dynamic, but it obviously will lead to wooden poems, at best, if the writers don't disguise or eliminate the structural supports of the double prompt. Compare these two drafts of the same poem from my notebook.

I used to skip stones in the water,
I once walked barefoot even the sharpest shoreline.
Now I find the nearest rock
And sit there. I let the tide come to me.

The child skips stones and runs
Barefoot on the sharpest shoreline.
His father finds the nearest rock and sits:
Unlike his child, the tide will always come to him.

Preformatted strategies risk imposing a limited mind-set on the author, so I favor discussing the concept, showing plenty of examples—again, lots of short poems—and discussing where the fulcrum appears in each of these models. Then I ask the students to write poems with fulcrums.

When students have an easy time recognizing the fulcrum and writing their own single-fulcrum poems, one might challenge them to consider the notion of a poem that has two or more fulcrums. Is it possible to write such a poem? Or do the conventions of poetry (or the limitations of human perception) dictate that a reader will be able to distinguish only one major turning point in a poem?

This conversation might go beyond the principles of poetry to questions of perception in general. Is it true that the largest number of objects one can perceive without actually counting is five? Does the mind break larger numbers of objects into smaller groups, groups of five or fewer? Is it true that infants see upside down? What is the difference between walking with one eye covered and walking with both eyes open? Can a line of poetry contain more than fourteen syllables before the reader unconsciously breaks it into two lines or more?

Imitation Versus Influence

What are your favorite poems and who are your favorite poets? How many of these poems and poets have you shared with your students? I once thought that if I simply mentioned a title or a poet, my students would search out that work! Then I realized that reading the poem aloud to the students would ensure that they acquired some knowledge of the poem. Now I think that the best way to reinforce shape, form, and voice is to read the poem aloud, *while the students follow the text*, or to ask *them* to read the poem aloud. Of course, one's choice of reader—that reader's skills and, admittedly, mood at the time—will greatly influence how the poem is received and perceived.

Any poem worth bringing to class I want the students to *hear*, to sense the rhythms and the ways a word can be held in the mouth like cotton candy on the tongue. It doesn't last forever but you've got a choice with every syllable whether to swallow, chew, or seek to prolong, to spit out or muffle, to emphasize the hiss or suppress each s.

Any poem worth bringing to class I also want them to *see*, for its shape has significant impact on the reader, just as the design of a printed advertisement makes the difference whether a reader actually pays attention to the words. The conventional shape of "Fourth of July," for instance (see Chapter 2), may say something about the seriousness of the subject. Imagine or copy the same poem "on center." Does this make a difference in how you approach the page? What if the poem were printed in the shape of a circle?

Keep the discussion of each poem brief, do not feel compelled to analyze the rhyme scheme and meter of every poem, and being sure to offer plenty of short, accessible poems, refer students to a librarian or bookseller to find more of their favorite poets' work.

It is almost impossible for a young writer not to be influenced, in some way, by the work of a favorite author. This influence may be immediate or long-delayed, conscious or unconscious. And it may involve choice of subject, a particular aspect of style, the use of favorite words or images, or any other component of poetry. It may arise in parody, out of loathing and disgust or out of love—but I doubt it can arise from indifference.

Style and Approach

The actual process of writing a poem has an enormous effect on its style. The author's attitude toward the subject, the author's mood, even the physical environment and the author's *physical* attitude will make a difference. How the author sets up or spontaneously responds to the environment are components of approach. Ask your students to imagine the difference in their writing if they were using a quill pen in the tower studio of a Renaissance castle, and to write that kind of poem as well as one written in a beatnik's pad, or in a teenager's bedroom today.

Consider the difference between listening to a piano concerto and listening to punk rock. Consider the difference between swaying to a waltz and bouncing to a fox-trot. I often play the radio when I write, accepting the random musical choices that are made for me and later wondering if a great critic will someday review my work, speculating what was playing on WNCS when I wrote or revised a certain line. Sure I'm presumptuous, but these little fantasies aren't hurting anyone and sometimes they amuse me, even keep me writing!

Equally important to the atmosphere in which one writes are the tools one uses. I *have* written poems in crayon and scratched words in the sand. I have written a first draft in cold type, setting the print by hand as the poem's language unfolded. The contrast between that painstaking, slow-motion process and the use of a 300 Megahertz Super 6.3 word processor is enormous, and might well result in poems of dramatically different length! Allen Ginsberg often captured his linguistic flow on a dictating machine, then later transcribed and revised those words into poetry on the page. Each of these approaches is valid and should be explored by poets of all ages.

For most writers, the infinite combination of variables settles into ritual with occasional side trips. Even the selection of a pen over a pencil, the choice to compose into a notebook instead of on a loose sheet of paper, the insistence on a BIC round stic medium blue ballpoint as the pen of choice and an eighty-page, lined, university notebook (sewn through the middle, mottled green, cardboard cover) make a big difference!

Once tools and setting have been established, our consideration turns to style. Will the language be formal ("Your touch, your kiss, have set my world on fire") or throwaway ("When I think of you I start to sweat")? Will end words rhyme; will the poem establish a regular meter? Will it paint a pic-

THE CHART OF INFINITE VARIABLES

VOICE OF NARRATOR	OBJECTS USED AS SYMBOLS
__ infancy __ just figuring out the world __ still counting toes __ young and in love __ starry-eyed __ ambitious __ ruthless __ heartless __ repentant __ "born again" __ cynical __ reflective __ all-knowing __ distant __ objective __ _____ _{your choice}	What's available for sale, or what do people construct or grow or use as tools at the time implied by the poem?
	SYMBOLIC RELATIONSHIP OF THESE OBJECTS EXAMPLES: clock, calendar, diary, meal, ceremony, ritual, song, tears, boxes, suitcases, bookshelves, disposable items, etc.
	PLACE Describe, evoke, or imply?
PERSON __ first __ first plural __ third __ third plural **Experiment with second person:** does it evoke the imperative mood?	**THE SENSES** **What senses are evoked by** the place, the objects, the time of action, the persons in the poem?
TIME OF ACTION __ past __ present __ future __ historical present Verb tense does not necessarily need to agree with the time of action!	**Never forget the evocative power of** smell, touch, taste and sound, as well as that of sight!

Figure 4–1. *The Chart of Infinite Variables*

ture or paint a picture *and* evoke a feeling? Will it seek to inform? Will it take a distinct physical shape? Will it be written with stronger concern for the sound of the words than for their appearance on the page? Will it emphasize certain sounds? Will it paint *and* evoke *and* tell a story? Will it use repetition? Any complete sentences? Will exclamation points (one student called them "commotion marks"!) and question marks be abundant, used sparingly, or will all sentences be declarative? Will the narrator use active voice only? Will the poem have dialogue?

These are all variables of style, and they only begin to suggest the range of choices at a poet's disposal. It isn't that a reader is going to say: "Oh look! Here's a poem in the third person, historical present, with a natural cadence of short, declarative sentences interspersed with brief exclamations." But the awareness of these options can inform the composition and revision of poems. Playing with them is half the fun!

Haiku and Lunes

At their simplest, *haiku,* a versatile short form with an honored tradition, are untitled, unrhymed, three-line poems, in English usually seventeen syllables long with five-syllable first and final lines that sandwich a line of seven syllables. This Japanese and Chinese form addresses a condition of nature that is almost inevitably linked, though subtly, to an element of human nature, as in the haiku of high school poet Erin Kern.

> Sitting in my tree
> I am more than just myself,
> Taller than the world.

But who's to say a writer must adhere to convention? Adult poet Ron Padgett's haiku refuses to involve nature in any way.

> First: five syllables
> Second: seven syllables
> Third: five syllables

Student Beverly Flemer gives her haiku a title, saving syllables in the haiku proper:

> **Freedom**
>
> The leaf appears dead
> Yet it tumbles to the ground
> every motion planned

One might also argue that a haiku can be titled *and* ignore the length requirements. Just pretend that such a poem, translated into Japanese or Chinese, *would* fit the traditional form! This is what happens in a *lune*, a three-line haiku hybrid in a pattern, depending on the author, of 3/5/3 words or 3/5/3 *syllables*. Some poets take even greater liberties with this still-evolving form, even changing how it is spelled. Steve Peterson and Ben Buckley, authors of two of the following lunes, were Verandah Porche's students.

> **Loon**
> *Steve Peterson*
>
> Light is captured
> In a stamped, marked envelope
> To send away

Tiny moments are made big in such poems:

> **Loon**
> *Verandah Porche*
>
> Can't open my
> mascara, Emily screwed it so tight
> no more tears

> **Roommates**
> *Ben Buckley*
>
> Four white walls
> two woodenly plastic desks
> two alien lives

Calling a lune, or some variation thereof, a haiku may offend some readers, but it's the writer's baby, so the writer can call it whatever he or she wants. Take heart from these entries in The Teachers & Writers *Handbook of Poetic Forms*, edited by Ron Padgett.

> To write a haiku that sounds traditional, make sure it shows the reader something to look at or hear or smell or taste or touch, and let it have three lines with the first and last a bit shorter than the middle. Do not add words to fill out the pattern. As with any kind of poetry that interests you, read lots of examples by many poets. (1987, 91)

> It is important to read a large variety of good lunes aloud, noticing the details as you go, so that you are brought into a closeup on each word and also into a 3/5/3 mental rhythm. One junior high school girl wrote 120

lunes in one night. During a period of protracted involvement, the mind can develop temporary mental molds for thought so that every idea or sight comes 3/5/3. (1987, 108)

Limerick

This marvelous form demonstrates the importance of rhythm and rhyme, which are so ingrained in the limerick that it is more easily taught by example, through its sound, than by definition. Tell a bunch of students that a *limerick* is two lines of rhymed anapest (three beats of iambic pentameter) followed by a rhymed couplet of two beats per line, and concluded with another anapestic line that rhymes with lines one and two, and you might as well be addressing a pile of bricks. Far more effective is to provide some examples and then to discuss what they have in common.

> Da da ta, da da ta, da ta
> Da da ta, da da ta, da ta
> Da da ta da dum,
> Da da ta da dum,
> Da da ta, da da ta, da ta.

> There once was a fellow named Bill
> Who swallowed a nuclear pill.
> The doctor said "Cough!"
> The darn thing went off,
> And they picked up his head in Brazil.

No one is sure where the limerick originated. One theory is that soldiers returning from France brought it to the Irish town of Limerick in 1700. Another theory points to *Mother Goose Melodies for Children*, published in 1719, and to several limericks published shortly thereafter. Edward Lear (1812–1888) is renowned for establishing the limerick as an instrument of nonsense and comical verse, but many of his limericks fail to snap us with a sharp twist in the last line, a device that has characterized the best limericks since his time. The simplicity of Lear's limericks, however, endears them to us and makes them memorable.

> There was an Old Lady whose folly
> Induced her to sit on a holly,
> Whereon, by a thorn,
> Her dress being torn,
> She quickly became melancholy.

There was a Young Lady of Poole,
Whose soup was excessively cool;
So she put it to boil
By the aid of some oil,
That ingenious Young Lady of Poole.

Limericks can follow Lear's tradition of starting each verse with "There was . . . ," but exceptional limericks will probably explore a more immediate way to start the poem. The first of Lear's limericks cited above is probably the better of the two because the last line explores a new rhyme and advances the narrative, rather than settling on repetition that results in a poem with only four lines of information.

Limericks are often bawdy jokes, off-color poems whose delight is in rhythm and rhyme being employed for naughty purposes.

A limerick packs laughs anatomical
Into space that is quite economical.
But the good ones I've seen
So seldom are clean,
And the clean ones so seldom are comical.

In ironic contrast to its use as the structure of bawdy jokes, the limerick is also a favorite format of nursery rhymes, sometimes in mildly disguised forms.

Little Bo-peep has lost her sheep,
    And doesn't know where to find them;
Leave them alone, and they'll come home,
    Bringing their tails behind them.

Little Miss Muffet
Sat on a tuffet,
Eating her curds and whey;
There came a spider,
Who sat down beside her
And frightened Miss Muffet away.

The man in the moon
Came down too soon,
And asked his way to Norwich;
He went by the south,
And burnt his mouth
With supping cold plum porridge.

Implicit in the limerick's rhyme-and-rhythm-associated-with-humor is a challenge: Can anyone write a limerick that does not seem to be trying for a laugh? Is a serious limerick possible? How can one take that familiar "da da ta, da da ta, da ta" rhythm and mute it sufficiently that the words of a poem create a somber response? How about a limerick on the subject of death?

The Sonnet

It may come as no surprise, by now, that I favor the broadest possible definition and application of any given poetic structure. Against all reason, I have sometimes defined as "rhyming" any two words that have the same number of syllables. Thus, *radar* rhymes with *carefree*.

Likewise, I favor an all-inclusive definition of *sonnet* as a fourteen-line poem. Yes, certain sonnets may follow a more prescriptive form, and students deserve the fun and occasional awe derived from reading sonnets so strictly conceived, as well as those with a more relaxed approach to the form.

Traditional sonnet forms include rhymed patterns of lines written in iambic pentameter. Most often, the first eight lines of the poem (an *octave*) set up a situation and the final six lines (a *sestet*) provide resolution, an ideal setup for the placement of a poem's fulcrum. But the variety of acceptable alternatives is almost infinite, ranging from three quatrains followed by a couplet to a seemingly arbitrary grouping of stanzas of different lengths or a single-stanza block of fourteen lines. In "Grandma Season," student Emily Coutant explores a traditional, rhymed sonnet form.

> My grandma sits under the locust tree.
> The flecks of green leaves flutter in her eyes.
> I wonder if her thoughts are caged or free.
> Her words dissolve; her heart is in disguise.
> She takes the lilacs in her fragile hands
> and holds them to her face. Is she recalling
> when grandpa tried to make her understand
> his love with a huge bouquet of lilacs falling
> in her lap? How can I know her mind?
> She floats like clouds across the vast, live sky.
> I wear her watch; her time is unconfined,
> by numbers, hands, elastic bands, or size.
> Her face wakes up like springtime when we sing.
> Someday I might wear her wedding ring.

The sonnet's form can be approximated or altered, and the piece can still feel like a sonnet, as in the following poem by Amy E. (Mia) Adams, who was a high school student when she wrote it.

Bouts Rimes

It is not an operatic phantom
that rakes
my coals and who at random
stokes the flames, makes

following temptation simple
obligation. He's forged my sacrificial dotted line, waived
everything but a dice roll's chance of resistance.
His quirk's the dimple
in the smile I'm slaved

to when offered to put aside my reasons.
He's pickpocketed my shame. I deliver
myself to evil. Using salts, wax, and witches' seasons
he soups the moon into a sliver

and sews my heart to my sleeve . . .
what sublimity tasting the weave.

Villanelle

Originating in sixteenth century France, a *villanelle* is a six-stanza poem whose first stanza contains three lines, the first and last of which repeat alternately as the final line of four ensuing three-line stanzas, and ending with a four-line stanza whose last two lines are the repeated lines:

1/2/3
4/5/1
6/7/3
8/9/1
10/11/3
12/13/1/3

It takes its name from a poem entitled "Villanelle," which introduced the form, using a rhyme scheme of 1/2/1 until the final, four-line stanza, which rhymes 1/2/1/1. Here is that first villanelle, by Jean Passerat, translated from the French by Mary Logue.

I have lost my dove:
Is there nothing I can do?
I want to go after my love.

Do you miss the one you love?
Alas! I really do:
I have lost my dove.

If your love you prove
Then my faith is true;
I want to go after my love.

Haven't you cried enough?
I will never be through:
I have lost my dove.

When I can't see her above
Nothing else seems to do:
I want to go after my love.

Death, I've called long enough,
Take what is given to you:
I have lost my dove,
I want to go after my love.

And here is one by student Tara Howe:

Alone

Please do not leave me here tonight
For I have no desire to be alone.
The groping hands of the venomous night

Try to catch me. In my line of sight
Are the shadows, moving with a chilling moan.
Please do not leave me here tonight.

The air has a destructive bite
That is tearing my soft soul. Crushed bones
From the groping hands of the venomous night.

I fear that I shall no longer be by morning light,
With my fallen body never to be known.
Please do not leave me here tonight.

In my struggle for life I will fight,
Yet the darkness will win with the lone,

Groping hands of the venomous night.
I warned you this would happen. Tight
Ropes pulling out my soul. Now to the surreal zone
With the groping hands of the venomous night.
Please do not leave me here tonight.

The repetition in a villanelle provides a sense of unity; the author's challenge is to find words that do not fall into the realm of predictability. Using homonyms and slight variations is one technique for keeping this predictability at bay.

Another strategy is to write a shorter villanelle, perhaps one having only four stanzas. I think I have seen this described somewhere as a *quadrille*.

Exercises

1. Write a short poem that sets up a strong contrast. Indicate where the fulcrum is.

2. Write a poem in the style or voice of a favorite poet. Do not be afraid of parody, should your pen take you in that direction.

3. Write a poem where the narrator's attitude comes through clearly. Remember that the persona of this narrator may be remarkably different from that of the author!

4. Write an autobiography composed of haiku, one haiku for each year of your life.

5. Create a series of limericks. See whether some of them can take the reader in a serious direction.

6. Write a sonnet and a villanelle. Which was easier? Why? Which gives you the most pleasure or chagrin? Why?

SCENES FROM A RESTAURANT

SQUEEZABLY SOLO
YOU CATCH WHAT HAPPENED TO BE MY EYE,
MUSICALLY YOU MOTION FOR ME
(AND MY LITTLE ONE)
TO JOIN YOU AT A TABLE FOR TWO,
CRAWLING ON HANDS AND KNEES
I BECKON MY WAITER TO SEND MY MEAL TO YOUR TABLE,
(MY LITTLE ONE) FOLLOWS WITHOUT:
HESITATION
FIRST, YOU GIVE ME LOOKS AND WHISPERS
THEN YOUR HAND VENTURES INSIDE MY SOUL . . .
WOW I NEVER,
AND THANKS FOR THE HAMBURGER
BUT CAN YOU COOK IT A LITTLE,
WELL,
WELL DONE?
NEXT (MY LITTLE ONE) IS KIND OF SWAYING
SUGAR, SWEET AND LOW, CAN YOU PASS IT TO ME?
I REALIZED THAT AFTER WE LEFT
YOU NEVER RETURNED MY MOTOR MOUTH MESSAGE,
AND (MY LITTLE ONE) CRIES FOR YOU EACH NITE
ALTHOUGH NOW, I SLEEP AROUND

▼

Here is both the entanglement of clarity, wordplay, and ill-defined meanings doubled with a restaurant and a one-night stand. This poem is not necessarily as clear as most of my others. Probably the most questionable example is "(my little one)," which I thought of as a number of things and could not necessarily pinpoint to be an object. Mostly, I think of it as a libido. However, I originally wrote the phrase thinking of a cat. So then I thought that if I could not decide, how could I expect the reader to agree with my decision?

This confusion is compounded by the use of exaggerations in the poetry. For example, it is outrageous to crawl on hands and knees to another table in a restaurant or impossible to have hands venture into someone's soul. Basically the choice of words was extended to enhance the mystery of the poem and create a specific scene.

—*Claire Feldman*

5

Longer and Lesser-known Forms

Yes, But Is It Poetry? The Prose Poem

The prose poem is a poem where the typesetter, not the poet, decides where to break the lines. Whereas poems are generally written in stanzas, prose poems are written in paragraphs. And, as in "Control," by student Molly Smith, the sentence, not the line, is the prose poem's basic unit.

> My stepmother worships the television just as she was taught to properly worship the holy trinity by her Roman Catholic upbringing. Her intense devotion spans all hours, and her knowledge of the religion reaches back to the days when color TV was just invented. Any fact, 1953 and beyond, ask it and she will know.
>
> She has her own trinity. The 45 inch entertainment center with surround sound and high fidelity color is the beginning. Resting and hidden like the holy ghost in the walnut cabinets to the left of the screen is her state of the art laser disk player.
>
> And her Jesus, her sweet savior that holds her hand through joy and conflict, is the remote control. We are not worthy enough, our souls not pure enough to touch it, so my brother and I wait for her to scan through channels, never presuming that we have any choice. It is all her, and she is tuned in to switch channels based on divine guidance.

One day I swear she will rise up and walk to the sea with her remote control, and just as Moses stood on the bank and asked God to save His people, my stepmother will part the waters as she types out the stations of the cross on her remote, and her slothful minions will follow, and be led to a new land.

Between my ipso facto, caveat emptor, laissez-faire definitions of poetry and prose poetry lies the unanswered question, "But how do you decide that what's presented as a poem is, indeed, poetry?" The answer to that is too personal, too subjective, for any one person to provide, at least in any authoritative fashion, for others. But, as a way of examining a group's diversity of opinion, asking each student to write out a definition of *poetry* is an eye-opening way to start a poetry course. To prove the fallacy of any given description of poetry, ask the students to write poems that illustrate and that contradict their definitions!

Sestina

A *sestina* has thirty-nine lines, the first thirty-six of which are organized in stanzas of six lines each. Each end word of the first stanza is repeated as an end word in each ensuing stanza in a prescribed sequence: 1,2,3,4,5,6; 6,1,5,2,4,3; 3,6,4,1,2,5; 5,3,2,6,1,4; 4,5,1,3,6,2; 2,4,6,5,3,1. The final stanza has three lines, each containing two of the end words, traditionally in the same sequence as in the first stanza: 1,2; 3,4; 5,6.

Like the villanelle, the sestina's form can be adapted to accommodate more relaxed standards. A "sestina" whose first stanza is only four lines long (is this a "quatrina"?) will thus be eighteen lines in length; a sestina with but a couplet for its first stanza will be just five lines long. Here, from my notebook, is perhaps the world's first coupletina.

Coupletina

She asked me if I knew which way the wind blew.
I squinched up my eyes and tried to seem knowledgeable

but I have a funny face that rarely looks knowledgeable
which is the main reason I'm always so blue.

A man who is knowledgeable and looks it never feels blue.

The longer the poem, the harder it is to create a piece that doesn't stall on the repeated words, a poem that truly moves forward. Here is one by Verandah Porche's student, Ben Buckley.

Sestina in Progress

The thick summer night falls;
a lemon moon
floats on rough water
while fishermen try to cast.
The humbug waves hide their fish
and even lovers are unlucky.

A young man on the pier pities the unlucky
fishermen. His hand slackens and a quarter falls
into the lapping waves where a fish
bobs to the top, curious about the new small moon.
His face breaks its smiling cast
and he walks away from the hungry water.

He reaches into his pocket to fish
out a cigarette. The light from the water
is as cold as the reflected moon.
This year has been unlucky:
first his job, and then his leg, and then he fell
in love with the nurse who set his cast.

She signed the cast,
"Love, Mia," while he ate the hospital fish.
His heart went straight over the falls,
and hit the cold water
hard at the bottom. He'd always been unlucky.
Her wedding band condemned him to moon

over her neat and tidy beauty. Her face, a smooth white moon,
still hangs in his mind's eye. The fishermen continue to cast
continuously unlucky.
The young man's skin is fish-
belly clammy. He stares at the turbulent water.
His foot, hovering over the gas, falls.

A solitary fish leaps from the water,
taunting every fallen and failed cast.
Tonight is a cruel moon, and everyone is unlucky.

What strategies does Buckley use to keep his sestina moving forward? What strikes me is that five of the six end words (*falls, moon, water, cast, fish*) are used as both nouns and as verbs. Used consistently as an adjective, *unlucky* is the only end word that serves as but one part of speech.

These little grammatical lessons require continual review; they should never be abandoned! Discussing sestinas provides a fine opportunity to review the parts of speech, and to ask students to make lists of nouns that work as verbs, and lists of adjectives that are sometimes used as nouns.

Joke Poems and Story Poems

My seatmate on a recent airplane trip was a professional, stand-up comedian. When I said that I write poems, he told me that he writes out his routines as free verse. "That way," he explained, "I can see the timing and phrasing of my lines."

I like to write joke poems as a way of remembering jokes I want to pass on to future generations. The joke poems in my notebook seem to grow stale faster than my other poems!

Two Men

An old man and his pal
are discussing, after dinner,
the effects of aging.

The old man's wife
is in the kitchen, washing dishes.
The old man's pal admits:

"My memory's starting to go."
"Not mine," says the old man, "I'm taking *a workshop*."
"A *workshop?* What's the name of this workshop?"

Old man thinks a minute,
then asks his friend:
"What's the name of that flower with the thorny stem?"

"A rose?"

"Thanks.
Hey Rose,
What's the name of that memory workshop I'm taking?"

As for story poems, they can always be presented as prose poems, though line breaks can provide infinite opportunities for startling transitions and unlikely juxtapositions. The best model for story poems may be Edward Field's *Variety Photoplays*, a series of poems based on movie plots. If you cannot find a printing of *Variety Photoplays*, many of the poems are collected in Field's *Selected Poems*.

Concrete Poems

In a sense all poems that are presented on the page are "concrete" poems because they have a physical shape. Strictly defined, however, a *concrete poem* is a poem where the shape suggests the focus of the poem or *is*, itself, the poem—in cases where the author has not used comprehensible language, but simply the characters of print or type to create a shape.

One might draw the U.S. flag, for instance, with *x*'s and *o*'s and call that a concrete poem (entitled "Old Glory"?), or create a peace symbol using words, as Grant Urie, a middle-school student of mine several years ago, did.

```
        world     If      peace
         the      you      of
          of      have    vision
        vision     a      super
         own      vision   own
          my       of       my
        That's    peace    That's
      pollution  Have  your    war
    without   landlord  lower  without
      world   your          lease  world
              a    It's    a
```

A science teacher, Ken Martin, who enrolled in a weeklong poetry workshop, wrote the concrete poem below for his father.

NTITLED

The purveyor of immortality
is a mortal. The subject smiles
at the one   who will not
be there   when   the
film is   developed.
My dad   took pictures
as I ran to   him laughing.
Then he left me with photos he
was never in to remember him by.

Mary Ellen Solt, a poet from Indiana, designs and sets type for her concrete poems, which do not always attempt to make a literal statement.

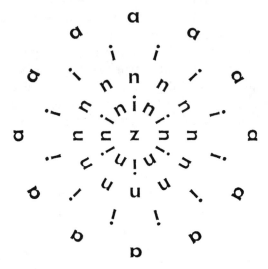

One of our best concrete poets, John Hollander, outlines the shape of the poem, then enters words to fill that shape, erasing the outline before typing up the final draft. Sandwiching a sheet of carbon paper between a fresh page of white paper and a newspaper photograph of then-President Nixon, I adapted Hollander's technique. I rolled the carbon-paper sandwich through my typewriter with the newspaper image facing me and the carbon paper aimed toward the clean sheet on the bottom. Wherever I decided the photograph was dark, I typed an X, leaving blank spaces wherever it was light.

The resulting carbon copy of the photograph showed me strings of X's where I could type words, and let me know which spaces to leave blank. After two or three days of mad fiddling, I had a poem that expressed my feelings toward our thirty-seventh President *and* that, from a distance, looked remarkably like him! I'm reprinting the poem, reduced to a fraction of its original size, which emphasizes its likeness to its subject and obscures (unless you have a magnifying glass) the actual words, which are pretty hateful.

This is old-fashioned technology, now that the same image can be scanned with dark and light spaces assigned, perhaps even the words filled in, by a desktop computer! Yet the slowing down required of the old technologies, typesetting by hand, retyping endless new drafts completely, or lettering the poem by hand with a special pen—these contemplative aspects of writing are swept away when we turn to computers.

Found Poems

In Ancient Times

In ancient times
aristocrats
sang the praises of bugs

and held competitions to see
who could best
identify their calls.

We are repulsed by some kinds of bugs
just like everyone else
but in some we see refined elegance as well.

As a way of demonstrating to a book discussion group in Brattleboro how everyday language can be interpreted as poetry, I recently recited the above words, which I'd lifted, nearly unedited, from an article in that day's *Brattleboro Reformer*. "Why that's Emily Dickinson," chirped one of the participants, before I had a chance to explain the poem's true source.

A *found poem* is language that was composed without "poetic intent." It is "found" by the person who first presents it as a poem, signing the work, with proper accreditation. According to custom, the finder of this language may not change any of the words or their sequence but provides the line breaks and is free to omit sections of the found language. The closer the original intent of the language comes to that of poetry, the less likely it is to qualify as true found poetry. The odd thing is how the found words seem to take on an added power when removed from their original context and presented alone.

During the war in Vietnam, poet Eric Torgersen found the following poem in a newspaper.

The Story of White Man Leading Viet Cong Patrol
AP Dispatch, Des Moines Register, August 4, 1968

The slain enemy resembled
an American Marine
who was 18 years old
when he disappeared.

The violent episode
was one of the strangest
in this strange war.

*

For a moment
the two young men—
the American Marine
and the white man
in the uniform of the enemy—
stared at each other.

*

"He had an AK 47
automatic rifle
but he just looked at me."

Gordon fired
after a moment's hesitation.

*

Several of the Marines suspect
that the unknown white man

whom they call "the Caucasian"
could have shot first
but deliberately held fire.

At the debriefing
everyone was afraid
to say what they had seen.

English Journal reprinted an equally chilling found poem from Julius Lester's *Search for the New Land: History as Subjective Experience* (1969, 3–4).

Parents
The New York Times, *February 7, 1968*

Linda failed to return home from a dance Friday night.
On Saturday
she admitted she had spent the night
with an Air Force Lieutenant.

The Aults decided on a punishment
that would "wake Linda up."
They ordered her
to shoot the dog
she had owned about two years.

On Sunday,
The Aults and
Linda
took the dog into the desert
near their home.
They
had the girl
dig a shallow grave.
Then

Mrs. Ault
grasped the dog between her hands and
Mr. Ault
gave
his daughter
a .22 caliber pistol
and told her
to shoot the dog.

Instead,
the girl

put the pistol
to her right temple
and shot herself.

The police said
there were no charges
that could be filed
against the parents
except possibly

cruelty
to
animals.

3-D and Kinetic Poems

Poetry as sculpture! Words carved into rock or hanging as mobiles or super-imposed on one another while a series of transparencies is laid down on an overhead projector. I can't show examples here because of the limitations of a standard, published book. But the spirit and principles of poetry, especially wordplay, can be captured off the traditional page, the expected poetic surface.

And consider the possibilities when the letters of words become animated, taking new shapes or new positions, forming new words. Kinetic poems may be created on advanced computer systems or on film, videotape, photographic slides shown in rapid succession, or in the form of a flip book, where the image is modified gradually, page by page, to create a sense of motion when the pages are riffled like a deck of cards.

Song

Using melody as a starting point, or adding melody after the words are written, or deriving both simultaneously is a joyous way to create poetry. Here's a collaborative song, really a twelve-line poem, written by Angelique Metivier, Erin Wintermeyer, Victoria Messer, Heather Graham, Eva Us, and Annie Williams, who were high school students at the time they wrote it.

My Father Is A Dentist

My father is a dentist; My mother is a nurse.
And when they are together, all they do is curse.
My school is like a prison; My courses really dumb.

Everyone around me thinks that I am scum.
I have no motivation. I have no basic skills.
To be this generation is like being killed.
Adult at twenty-one. Adult at eighteen.
When will we really know what adult means?
We can try to make it better. We do the best we can.
But this society won't try to understand.
We are simply products of our folks before.
So if you try to blame us, we'll only blame YOU more.

I recently worked with three electric guitar–whacking boys and a drummer in a songwriting class. They had improvised a hard-rock "melody" (more like a loud, rhythmic pattern, with alternating solos), and with just a little prodding devised the following lyric:

Time once lost has gone off course,
Feeting, fleeting.
Memories flowing from the same source,
Dreaming, dreaming.
Come into my little world and see what I am
Thinking, thinking.
Take my demons—exorcised and
Screaming, screaming.

The buses are coming, they're loading me in,
These are the wages of drinking and sin.
They're tying me up, they're taking me down,
They're running my soul right into the ground.
I can't stay . . .
Watching my soul go away!

Rhymed, Metrical, Blank, Syllabic, and Free Verse

Apart from the specific genres already listed, poems may be rhymed or written in a specific meter. The rhyme may be regular so the reader will hear the rhymed sounds at specific rhythmic points in the poem, or it may occur internally or haphazardly or perhaps even without the author's awareness! (Given the level of familiarity I believe poets should have with any poem they release for public consumption, this should be impossible, but I know—yes, from my own experience!—that writers can be surprised even by their own published poems.)

The regular rhyme and meter of a poem can highlight a mood, espe-cially when the intent is to provide a moment of humor, as in "Waiting for Summer," by high school student Jeanie Hudson.

> The classroom jumps, it wakes in fear.
> Teacher is mad; he has been all year.
> He does not understand why we drift to sleep
> While Calculus is taught; so fun, so deep.
> He does not remember the boredom, the bummer
> Of being in school and waiting for summer.

In *blank verse*, the author makes no attempt to rhyme, but creates a metrical pattern.

Syllabic verse is a more forgiving form of blank verse: The rhythms of meter may or may not be present as the author presents a line pattern deter-mined by the number of syllables (not beats) in each line.

Free verse, what Frost called "playing tennis with the net down," allows the author to ignore both the conventions of rhyme *and* of meter.

Using the Shape of the Page

The poet A. R. Ammons, borrowing from one of the Beat Poets, who'd writ-ten a novel on shelving paper so he wouldn't have to change pages in his type-writer, published *Tape for the Turn of the Year*, a book-length, skinny poem that is, essentially, a poet's journal from the days and nights surrounding the 1964 New Year, composed on an adding machine tape that he ran through his typewriter as one very long, very thin page, a continuous flow of paper.

Within months of publication of Ammons' book, several of his stu-dents had embarked on their own adding machine–tape poems. The length of the project, plus the fact that it tied up the typewriter, led to a sense that it's just as well to get this thing *done*, a freer attitude toward poetry than the students had brought to their shorter efforts.

Likewise, the constraints of other shapes, similar to the constraints of a concrete poem started by a physical outline, can inform the poem's content and style.

Exercises

1. Write a prose poem that starts with a small fantasy and explodes into a fully imagined scene.

2. Write a sestina, or a shorter poem that is based on the form of a sestina. Before starting, you may want to make a list of homonyms and words that can be used as more than one part of speech, or that have a variety of meanings. Such a list will provide a good resource for versatile end words!

3. Write a joke poem or a story poem. Think about your childhood adventures, and see whether something in your past, or your knowledge of someone else's past, can lead to a story poem or a ballad.

4. Write a concrete poem, inventing or borrowing the shape. This can be as simple as a poem that looks like a rectangle or that takes the shape of the surface on which it is written. Or it can be as complex as a poem that, from a distance, resembles a photograph!

5. Review a current newspaper in search of an article that can be edited into a found poem. Consider sources besides the newspaper. A shopping list? A note written on a balled-up scrap of paper? Messages to parents from the school?

6. Write a blues song. Using original or existing melodies, pay attention to the traditions of incremental repetition. Start with a simple line, repeat it in a pattern, with information added at key points in the melody. Does it work as a poem, or does it need to be accompanied by melody?

And Oh Palindrome And Oh

Oh and I don't know
what you mean
to me,
dagger heart, drench coat
drip,
your old fallacious
zip pal,
How ever
(should)
I know the run-arounds,
homebound fun.
The greedy pig that swallowed my pennies . . .
I lie still,
solemn, scared;
oh (how) to satisfy
And
Oh

▼

When I began this poem, I started first with the title, intending to
format the poem as a palindrome. The pun on the word palindrome
is also relevant here because a palindrome literally is a continuous
cycle of letters, plus, the narrator's frustration with the situation is a
cycle similar to that of a palindrome. Here the concept of a non-
faithful relationship is compared to the palindrome's never-ending
cycle. The best example of this is the first and last two words of the
poem that unite the physical structure of a never-ending palindrome
with the ideological thoughts of the poem.

The words in parentheses act as question marks, indicating the
narrator's indecisions and mixed feelings. The line breaks are intended to emphasize particular words. I believe that the poem is clear as
a whole, though some words, I must admit, I placed because they
sounded poetic and had a distant coherence to the situation I was
portraying. I am not sure if this is beneficial to the poem. I believe
that the strength of the poem is the pun on palindrome and the concept of cycles.

—Claire Feldman

6
Music and Wordplay
Breaking Rules and Breaking Lines

Music

Music! A student who learns early in life the music of language (nursery rhymes and songs heard prenatally, with the introduction of rhymed verse and free and blank verse in the elementary school years and wordplay throughout the human experience!) can soon learn to create songs, with and without melodies. Writing poems is as close as this marginal singer and guitar player can come to the experience of making "serious" music, and I believe the creative high I feel in those lucky moments is one of life's best experiences. What trouble would I be making with all this excess energy if somewhere along the line I hadn't picked up a love of words, the pleasure of carrying on in a long-winded, one-sided conversation or a blazing flash of blue inspiration emerging from the silken point of my BIC round stic medium?

For years I did this to the accompaniment of a stereo, but more recently I've preferred the sounds of life around me, right now a late-August wind in the leaves of soft maples that surround our yard, the occasional rattletrap whacking along the dirt road that passes our rutted driveway.

For students I'd want to emphasize the music in language and the possibility that such music might be tapped by having some favorite radio station blaring in the background. Classical or pop music, rap, the blues, country, and almost anything else on FM and AM radio can tell us a lot about the importance of form. Repetition (of words or sound, even rhyme), the repetition of rhythm, the repetition of melody, all these strategies can inform the writing of poems.

Ask your students to transcribe the lyrics to a favorite song, and spend time with the words, a strange switch for those who have only heard the lyrics with a melody! In many cases, students will decide the lyrics *need* the melody! Can a rhyme scheme be diagrammed? Do the rhythms of the words come through, even without the music? What tricks are used to stretch words or alter the rhythms?

Wordplay Is Not Just Nonsense

There's a story about a local arts council that was about to close its doors. Deep in debt, volunteer trustees abandoning ship, the council's director nervously approached a loyal patron, a woman who had donated $500 three years in a row, and asked for $20,000, enough to erase the organization's debt. No dummy, the patron was about to decline, asking, "Who else have you approached?"

The director stammered, "No one. We're putting all our begs into one ask it."

And, the story goes, the patron, still wiping tears of laughter from her eyes, wrote a one-time-only check for $20,000!

Wordplay may not always result in such serendipity, but its practice, from the use of homonyms and puns to the discovery of spoonerisms to Pig Latin to talking backwards to anagrams to rhyming to secret codes, reinforces the sense of language as both tool and toy. Rap music, lyrics driven by rhythmic necessity (if not thoughtful tenderness), provides an example.

Inventing their own languages or experimenting with the sounds of our existing language, students explore the complexity and variety of a tool that provides opportunity for outright statement or implication, assertion or nuance, dejection or joy, sincerity or sarcasm, congratulations or condemnation, laughter or tears.

Wordplay doesn't necessarily invite laughter. It can evoke noble intentions, can serve to convince, as in John Kennedy's memorable double-imperative, "Ask not what your country can do for you; ask what you can do for your country!" In such instances, one can imagine that the elegant expression was actually teased from a more prosaic statement: "We should ask what we can do for our country, not what it can do for us," perhaps revised to, "We shouldn't ask what our country can do for us, but what we can do for it" to

"Don't ask what your country can do for you; ask what you can do for it," then polished into its final form.

Wordplay can be obvious, as in the arts director's unintentional spoonerism. It can be subtle, as in Kennedy's exhortation. It can also be subliminal, almost invisible. In the following poem, wordplay is at its most obvious in the joke, lines seven through nine, built on parallelism (". . . like stars, like debutantes,/ "like false teeth,/ we come out"), and in a subtler suggestion of spoonerism ("bound by worlds . . . blinded by words") and the half-spoonerism ("blood guess" stated, "God bless" implied).

The Moon

lasted all night & seemed to burn
toward noon
after just that brief blue darkness
nightfall bound by worlds.

And we turn to that rising
again & again
we turn and like stars, like debutantes,
like false teeth
we come out.

How would we know
blinded by words

as we are

the blood guess of morning on the rocks
how it dawns on the gulls
creak of their throats against salt wind.

As the author of this poem, my half-spoonerism delights me, yet I doubt that a single reader of that poem has ever contemplated the possibility that "blood guess" is intended to suggest "God bless." I *am* a tiny bit disappointed that no one has mentioned this clever wordplay; I'm simultaneously pleased that my moment of genius is working its magic without the reader's conscious awareness. It's the equivalent of one of my secret codes from childhood.

Sometimes I wonder whether unusually slow readers are more likely than average and fast readers to discover the hidden possibilities in language. As a reader whose slow pace has always seemed a burden, I wonder whether it hasn't had its compensating factors!

When I come upon puns, I sometimes try to build little jokes around them, as in the man who discovered that two hundred dollars for a wig was a "high price to pay." So, in another short poem, I stumbled on three puns, one reinforced by the line break ("you make me want to throw up/ my hands in delight"), another in the homonym of "delight" and "the light," and another a little linguistic "a ha!" that unfolded as I wrote the last line: to "hold fire" one might either be cupping flames or refraining from pulling the trigger.

Comet Come

If I could make clear
Come Heaven streaking blue light stronger than sun's
If I could wipe the stains off retina
& iris & we could gaze & gaze
Into each other's silent vision.

Clouds hang on mountain tops here for days
They seal us out. Yet the hardest knowledge
Came one cloudless night
I saw a shooting star
& tried to show it to my friend.

How difficult to share perceptions
While they are still intact!
Is it divine protection (perfection?)
That delays the shutter,
Keeps the deer in front of the bullet?

I want to test thatmospheric freeway
You burn through, Want to know
Can you warm us in time
& close the holes behind you.
Will you draw the oceans up & over us as prophesied in Luke?

If I could only share your unlikely flowering
Instead of riding this downward slump
Like a country out of oil, jerking still.
Like a casket lowering,
You march your mystery through my mind

Light years compacted in the briefest flash.
You make me want to throw up
My hands in delight, ask man
To perform the incredible
Like hold fire.

These instances of wordplay did not occur to me as I was chewing the end of my pen in a mental search for a nifty pun to write a poem around; they emerged as part of a string of words, themselves emerging in response to the feelings or images evoked by their predecessors. I don't believe that the feeling must necessarily come first in the writing of a poem; it is often discovered within the poem's first three or four lines, or it otherwise evolves as the poem develops. Perhaps the best poems, within their first three or four lines, wrest from their author the prevailing mood that was brought to their creation, and assert themselves in spite of the writer's original intention.

I do not usually write poems around clever slogans or bits of discovered word play, but use my notebook as a repository for any forms of wordplay I may come across as my mind habitually flips the language around. The final pages of my latest notebooks are filled with spoonerisms and backwards words and phrases that, like a squirrel burying nuts in the fall, I have stored. Maybe some day I'll dig them up for use in a poem or story. As fresh and original as these discoveries are to me, I'm certain that hundreds or thousands of other writers have also entered many, if not all of them, into *their* notebooks.

It's always a pleasure for me to happen upon these funny quirks of our English language, recognizing that *embargo* backwards is "o grab me," that *catatonic* is "cannot attack," that *revolution* (phonetically) is "no shoe lover," *Subaru* is "you're a bus," *diaper* is "repaid," and that *dermatitis* is "sit tight, I'm red." Like a small percentage of other U.S. citizens, for some unknown reason I taught myself to speak backwards when I was in high school. Pig Latin just wasn't enough!

And glancing over my copious lists of spoonerisms, I see that *grilled cheese* is "chilled grease," that *hat fled* is "flat head," that *shock of criticism* is "crock of sh . . . icism." Maybe these entries will never be used. Probably they won't be. But in some way the act of writing them down reinforces their presence, makes them harder to forget, and at various moments of conversation, or in composing a poem on language, or perhaps while I'm raising funds for an arts organization, they'll burst through. In "Introduction," I create a mad professor who insists that language *and* time are actually running backwards, ranting:

> catatonic is cannot attack, and revolution is no shoe lover.
> I can say whole sentences backwards
> without prior consideration, accurate
> unless you work one up ahead of time
> to trick me. Language loved and played with
> like a child
> reveals itself.

Realizing, finally, that no one will take him seriously, he becomes alternately bitter and plaintive:

> Except on film we never see it that way
> because of seeing upside down at birth.
> Oh, never mind, you're too stupid anyway.

> But can't you just see the sense of pieces flying back together,
> the compost recomposing into real banana peels,
> the banana reentering your body to put it politely as I can
> and being undigested, unchewed, and emerging
> from your mouth only to have the peel replaced,
> the whole thing plunged back into the paper bag
> and driven backwards to the supermarket
> where eventually it is untugged to Costa Rica
> and hung back on the tree,
> which resorbs it as it goes from green to whatever they are before
>   then.

> Meanwhile, presidents and kings are unwaging wars
> and back away from their jobs
> which fall into the laps of those who are ready to retire.

Form

A poem's form can run from concrete to free verse to a specific, traditional pattern, such as a haiku or sonnet. Each traditional form offers its own, special advantages, from the clarity or efficient irony inherent in haiku to the gathering of linguistic energy and powerful rhythms in the sonnet and longer forms. But even free verse poems have a "form." That form may be unique to the poem in question, but it is, nevertheless, a form. The form of a didactic free-verse poem like "Introduction," for instance, might include its lecturelike cadence, the rhetorical repetition of a line or phrase, or the extension of a central idea or image.

Persona and the Power of Voice

Coupled with form is voice: An extreme example is the limerick and the voice it automatically implies. In the absence of traditional form, the voice a free-verse poet applies has immense bearing on each free-verse poem. Each free-verse poem has the opportunity to create its *own* voice, without the expected tone inherent to certain forms. The voice of "Introduction" is that of the earnest, but deranged, "mad professor," desperate to communicate a latest theory. Creating such voice involves the use of persona, a personality not obviously that of the author.

In Chapter 8, I mention Dave Smith's advice that, when asking students about their poems, one should keep the focus on *the narrator*, not "you, the author." This approach provides a comfort zone for the author. More important, I think, it reminds the author that today's narrator may be a completely different person from tomorrow's. Taking on persona, I believe, is basic to writing a meaningful range of poetry.

Think of it as playwrighting! Each new poem may be a speech for a new character in a play. A single poem may use more than one voice. It may become, eventually, a three-act play! Indeed, as explained in the Introduction, students deserve opportunities to perform poems, enhancing images with movement and sound, exploring attitudes from parody to high tragedy. A lively anthology, *I Feel a Little Jumpy Around You*, edited by Naomi Shihab Nye and Paul B. Janeczko, collects poems in pairs, one written by a male and the other by a female, excellent starting points for students who want to experiment with contrasting voices.

As much as we encourage students to write with voice, I would argue that *the reader* bears half the responsibility for finding voice in a poem or other literary endeavor. The reader must assume ownership of the poem, rather than the intimidation often associated with poetry or school reading. Knowing that the reader has this opportunity or responsibility may impel some writers to create works so clear, so strong, that they defy misinterpretation!

Reminded that the poems they write do not need to reflect their own experiences, attitudes, and voice, students sometimes have greater success exploring substantive issues than when they feel responsible for representing only their own point of view.

To help students understand the range of voices they might employ, I often have them brainstorm a list of characters—by profession, by hobby, by obsession, by personal circumstance—and have them write from the point of view of one of those characters, for example a former doctor who collects race cars and was paralyzed during a weekend racing accident. A poem she might write on freedom, for instance, might be quite different from what a teenage student would write. Her metaphors (possibly expressing a doctor's power turned to helplessness) would be unique! Indeed, the poem she might write before her accident would be quite different from the poem she'd write after the event.

Breaking the Rules

The power of a voice often tempts the writer to rethink the rules of grammar. Some writers find that conventional English or the presence of punctuation marks mars an intentional ambiguity or creates a visual intrusion. Equally important, wordplay can be enhanced by an awareness of the conventions and a healthy understanding of how to break those rules.

> Language loved and played with
> like a child
> reveals itself.

The absence of a comma, either following *with* or *child*, leaves to the reader whether the middle line modifies "played with" or "reveals itself." That intentional ambiguity provides "reader's choice."

> and laugh and swear
> we'd never come so close
> to getting caught

The contraction *we'd* in the second line leaves to the reader the decision whether *we would* or *we had* is intended. Is the narrator saying that "we promised ourselves to be more careful next time" (*would*) or "we agreed that this was the closest call ever" (*had*)?

Again, it doesn't matter so much whether the reader or critic notices these clever moments; as long as they amuse the author and do not distract the reader, they are probably contributing to the appeal of the poem.

As comforting as it may be to some writers to contemplate a form of verbal expression where breaking the rules is sometimes preferable to following them, other writers are terrified by a territory where the guidelines have been erased. Sentence fragments. Sentences, often run-on sentences, where the author, in an obvious attempt to show off, has prolonged the expression beyond a reader's tolerance, perhaps delaying the imposition of a verb or subject until the very end, dragging along a curious but unhappy reader who simply wishes the narrator would get on with the show, great extravagant spillings of language, effusions and spleen bleeding, the gawking descriptions of or from a life someone else is living, the question how they could let things get that way, the pure explication of one or more of the senses applied to the magical and often unobserved world: Sentences, in grammatical as well as in prison terms, can be long or short.

What has no one else written about? How many prepositions can you find to end a sentence and still keep it logical? (The best I've heard: "Why did you bring those books I don't want to be read to out of up for?") What tricks of language has no one ever used? In those territories there *are* no rules. Yet one can never know whether these are truly uncharted spaces; one has never read it all.

But to live outside the law you must be honest, and for most of us, knowing the rules is essential if we're gonna break them. So I take issue with the assumption that poetry is writing without rules. The rules are suspended perhaps, but they're there. Their power to create tension, even a reader's impatience or anger, is not, I maintain, a license to allow misunderstanding. And this is why the author needs to know the rules—to be able to recognize where misunderstanding may occur and whether it's worth the risk.

e e cummings broke the rules and doing so created a form that has been widely imitated, perhaps even in the *Archie & Mehitabel* series by Don Marquis. Archie, a cockroach, types letters to Mehitabel, the cat, by diving headfirst onto each typewriter key. Because he cannot hold down the Shift key at the same time he's diving at a letter, Archie cannot capitalize anything, so his references to himself are, à la cummings, in the lower-case *i*.

Learning the rules of grammar and punctuation is a lifetime process, but fascination with their structure is not common to all literate people. Is it possible that more of us would develop this important concern if grammar and punctuation were taught a little differently? Rather than just crafting complete sentences, what if students were asked to create an incomplete sentence for every complete one they wrote? In the resulting work, are the same feelings/ideas/information expressed?

What is the effect, in a poem or story, of omitting quotation marks when a character is speaking? How about doing away with paragraph indentations as well? Can words within dialogue be intentionally misspelled, even if the quotation marks are omitted?

What are the advantages a poem offers when one wants to break the rules? Line breaks can serve as punctuation. The scattering of words on a page or the clumping of phrases in a way that makes sense *and* carries visual impact create situations where suspension of the rules is necessary and therefore justified. Even the title of student Justin Briggs' "A Conversations" thumbs its nose at convention.

```
                    one.
        Her face, contorts in a
                slow lock
                    She crosses her
                i's and t's
        and slips, a glance into my cup,
                        two.
        She drops, her eyes
                        and sends, frowns
                    thru the plastic
        cup, and into, my head
        where it, creases in fright
        i cry out, in shock!
                        as feeling my legs, lift i
        drip
                    off                    [three.]
                    my chair and
                onto: the floor (into: her arms)
        where I am at last
                    able to: go,
                    asleep.
```

Breaking Lines

For writers who are hesitant about the use of line breaks, let me provide a simple chart that lists a variety of strategies for breaking lines in a poem. Following any of these strategies can reveal little secrets that are buried in our language. The writer of a syllabic poem may find, in revising, a need to hyphenate a word such as *therapist,* to hold one syllable in the upper line, while shifting the final two syllables to the following line, and thus discover that *therapist* is "the - rapist."

Writing in a particular rhythm often frees up the imagination to the point where dynamic statements of rhetorical power are created. Lines can be broken where the author sees the opportunity to create a surprise or apparent contradiction or ambiguity:

> we just couldn't get along
> without him

or

HOW TO BREAK LINES IN POETRY WRITING

"Enjambment is the running of a thought from one line to the next without a break in syntax"

1. SYLLABICS

Establish patterns or keep the same number of syllables in every line. It's easy to count syllables by drumming them out on a table top. Write the number of syllables for each line right next to that line. Look for patterns and revise the poem to emphasize their effect.

2. RHYTHM

Establish a certain rhythm through metrical or syllabic patterns. This is similar to making lyrics for a melody that has already been written. Try thinking up lines while jogging or while doing something else that is rhythmic and automatic. Or try writing while listening to a march or a waltz.

3. FOR HUMOR, SURPRISE OR OTHER EFFECT

Make line breaks where necessary to establish certain effects. Some stand up comedians write their routines out like poems so they can "see" the timing of certain lines.

4. TO UNDERCUT THE MEANING OF THE LINE THAT IS BEING BROKEN, OR TO ESTABLISH AN IRONY OR CONTRADICTION

The line, by the way, should be considered an individual unit that contributes to the whole of the stanza or entire poem. Each good line should be able to stand on its own as an interesting bit of writing.

> The demolition derby featured drivers from all over
> The state. The crowd roared stupidly
> With you and me as the cars destroyed each other ...

The first line implies drivers from a wide geography, while the start of the second line undercuts that notion, implying the narrator's "gee whiz" naivete. Similarly, the narrator judges the crowd negatively in the second line, then in the third line is also roaring "stupidly." Would the rhythm of the third line be improved by omitting "the" to read:

> "With you and me as cars destroyed each other ..." ?

5. FOR PHYSICAL SHAPE

An extreme method is to draw an outline on a sheet of paper, then fill it with x's:

```
xxxxxxxxxxxxxxxxxxx
xxxxxxxxxxxxxxxxxxx
xxxxxxxxxxxxxxxxxxx
xxxxxxxxxxxxxxxxxxx
xxxxxxxxxxxxxxxxxxx
```

Substitute words for the x's to form a poem with a special shape. These can be very elaborate, mountains reflected in water, for instance, or even nearly photographic, in the same way that computers create photographic images using nothing but letters, numbers, or dots. Less dramatic, more common, and something everyone should learn, is just trying to write a poem whose shape, though abstract, is inviting. Poems are meant to be seen, and read aloud and listened to.

Poetry allows total freedom of verbal and visual expression. The idea is to experiment with the limitless possibilities to discover what makes the author happiest!

Figure 6–1. *How to Break Lines in Poetry Writing*

> I want you
> to get out of my life

Line breaks also impart physical shape on the poem and can be manipulated to achieve a variety of visual effects.

Exercises

1 Write poems as you listen to different kinds of music. Keep track of which poems were written with which music. When they hear a poem that was written while music was playing, can others accurately guess what type of music it was?

2. Create a piece of found poetry (see Chapter 5) where the line breaks enhance the drama of the language.

3. Here is a series of consecutive assignments. The students are asked to complete this exercise one step at a time, not knowing that a further assignment will be attached to each "draft" that results from the current challenge.

    a) Write a two-paragraph story;
    b) turn it into a poem;
    c) rewrite the poem allowing exactly ten syllables per line;
    d) rewrite the poem emphasizing a special physical shape.
    e) Start a completely new draft based on a single image or phrase from a previous poem. Begin each line or stanza of your poem with the same phrase or question, based on the selected image or phrase. Does this impart rhythm or shape?
    f) Rewrite the poem, incorporating some or all of the "start" words *within* some of the lines.

4. An exercise to bring out awareness of voice: Write a new poem where you consider the educational level of the narrator. What kinds of word choices will your narrator make? Who is the audience and how does this, like the narrator's educational level, affect word choice? What is the narrator's goal/purpose, and how does this affect word choice?

5. Write a poem without using punctuation. How can you guide a reader through the language without commas, question marks, quotation marks, and the other tools of punctuation?

6. Make lists of short words that have many syllables and long words
   that have few syllables, (e.g., *area* and *screeched*), then use them in
   poems to make very long lines that have few syllables and short
   lines that have many syllables.

Wham

While exhaling the essence of love
tempts the lonely . . .
watch bikini swimmers
flaunt cleavage at your TV screen,
tanning oil drips
into the crystal blue pool
while Sinatra
heaves
a tune in our ears,
the remote control
gets lost between
the cracks in the couch cushion
while retrieving another soda
from the kitchen to gulp without;
hesitation.
And I breathe out
the words of love . . .
love not for you
but for the afternoon
Baywatch series
so I can run my hands along the TV screen,
again
yelling at the beauty
of
media

▼

This poem is chock-full of substance. This is one of my favorite poems. The balance between clarity and mystery and wordplay is evident. The title is the motive of the poem, though it is not as explicit and only describes a mere noise. However, when I think of the word *Wham*, it seems to me to be in your face, loud. This description is what the media inflict upon our society. The poem is a mockery of this behavior.

I chose to mimic the simple event of watching a TV show. The exaggeration of movements and the examples emphasize the grossly commercial American role models. This poem is basically a short story. The language is quite simple, and the message is clear.

—*Claire Feldman*

7

Metaphor and Simile, Unmetaphor and Symbolism

Metaphor and Simile

To remember the difference between *metaphor* and *simile*, I still have to run Miss Clough's old mnemonic through my mind: "Simile . . . similar . . . like or as; Metaphor . . . no like or as." It *is* helpful to classify metaphors, but learning the difference between metaphor and simile is not nearly as useful as learning to recognize and to create metaphors of all kinds. Meanwhile, Miss Clough is drilling the students on defining the difference between a Petrarchan and a Shakespearian sonnet, or memorizing "Simile: like or as; metaphor: no like or as."

To reinforce the value of metaphor, I sometimes send students to the library on a metaphor hunt. In a half hour, list all the metaphors and similes you can find, in any of the books in the whole collection. Provide documentation that allows your reader to find the book and the metaphor you have listed. How will you organize your search? Will you first look up *metaphor* on the library's computer or card catalogue? Will you go straight to the literature section and start skimming the pages of obscure poets?

My own writing suffers from an absence of metaphor (a generic term I'll use henceforth to imply both metaphor and simile), so I'm trying to develop the use of spontaneous metaphor in my daily speech, looking for moments when, like a scout leader with the only flashlight at midnight, I can focus attention on the subject of my choice.

Imagine writing where the reader's lower teeth get scraped up a chalkboard! Words can do that. The potential of metaphor, described in its broadest sense, is to make things felt. I want the reader to feel and hear those teeth on the chalkboard, maybe even give off an involuntary shiver or utterance. I'd like to evoke pleasant sensations that are equally powerful, but without resorting to cliché, that seems harder to do.

Before sending students off on a metaphor hunt, I remind them that a metaphor is the comparison of two *things*. There must be a noun on each side of the equation: The pillow was an icy brick, *not* The pillow was icy as a brick. In the first example, *pillow* is compared to *brick*, two *things*. In the second example, what I call a *half metaphor*, an adjective occupies half the equation when *icy* is compared to *brick*.

Eighth-grade poet Michael Blouin recently published a poem in *Potato Hill Poetry* that provides a wealth of examples of metaphor, simile, and metaphoric language.

A Winter's Tale

The sky was an orange haze,
A blanket of rolling clouds
Peach colored and soft.

As I walk outside,
The sounds that greet me
Are the low tone wind
And the rattling arms of bare trees.

So I walk across my yard,
The light snow crunching beneath my boots,
I enjoy the silence and
Envy the night's calmness.

The air is cold,
The wind softly blowing at
My winter clothes.
My breath fumes out
Like a dragon's thick plume.

Snow lightly drifts from the sky.
Occasionally, the wind would pick up
And the snow would pelt down
As if an endless sea of confetti.

But the snow always returns
To its gentle, blustery own.
And I see the evergreen branches
With their muscles of snow.
And the sea of white,
The ocean of snow.

With this, I turn to go,
And head back to my house,
With its frosty windows
Glowing gently from the candles inside.

The peaceful scene is silent,
As I enter my house.
Yet I can't help thinking
That the scene I love
Is but a Christmas ornament.

Hanging on a bigger world's Christmas tree.
Small and glowing,
And I can't help seeing
A bigger world's child shake us
And restart the snowing.

And I wonder this to myself,
As I nestle in bed.

Part of the magic of Blouin's poem is the skillful set up of the first stanza, which puts the reader in a metaphorical mind-set. The following stanza, therefore, appears metaphoric, when (at least in the first three lines, "As I walk outside,/ The sounds that greet me/ Are the low tone wind") it actually presents outright fact, which is *then* extended into metaphor: "And the rattling arms of bare trees." For the rest of the poem, a reader may sense the tension between metaphor and outright statement.

Brainstorming and classifying metaphors can establish a mind-set for any writer who wants to nurture the habit of creating or seeing metaphor, so I sometimes write a bunch of headings on the board, including Metaphors, Similes, Half metaphors/Half similes. After carefully reminding them that proper nouns may not be used (important lest the offerings all be "So and so is a flake" or "So and so is like a rose"), I ask the students to call out metaphors as I deliberate under which heading each offering should go.

Metaphors

snowboarders are fruitcakes

liberty is a diamond

she was a busy bee

Similes

snowboarders are like fruitcakes

liberty is like a diamond

she was like a busy bee

Half metaphors

snowboarders are nutty as fruitcakes

liberty is precious as a diamond

she was busy as a bee

Here is a list of metaphors brainstormed by Darlene Johnson's eighth-grade students at Cabot School, in Cabot, Vermont.

My attitude is a strong wind, always changing directions but never changing heart.

My soul is a tadpole, swimming in a pond looking for a mother.

My leg is my heart. It feels pain when you prick it.

God is an anchor. When the world is rough, He keeps me in one place.

My brain is empty, not any different than a balloon.

My heart is a burning, crying, clawing baby dancing through life to old fogie music. My eyes are constantly crying cause they don't understand anything. They're subjected to this horrible world, doing the Niagara Falls deal. My feet are making me trip on my own mistakes, stupidity and self-hate, so I fall helplessly to the dirt you walk on, never to get up again.

Extended Metaphor

Extension often provides remarkable opportunity for detail, sometimes with humorous effect. Instead of "His nose was red" (mere description) or "His nose was red as a cherry," (a half metaphor), try to come up with an extended metaphor: "His nose was a fluorescent cherry. It lit his way from room to room as he enlightened each cluster of wedding guests on his latest theories. It seemed at once to sniff out the finest crepes, to light his way to the freshest bowl of punch."

Extending half metaphors is equally effective: "Busy as a one-winged bee with a dipper full of nectar." Suddenly the old cliché, "busy as a bee" takes on new luster because the author has elaborated, extended, the noun side of the equation. Jokes are often built on a form of extension, sometimes the extension of cliché: "Your teeth are like the stars . . . they come out at night."

Other Classifications

Some students may be interested in further classification, though at a certain point the definitions seem superfluous. One might recognize *adverbial simile*, where a noun *and* verb are compared to the other half of an equation. In "He talked like a machine gun," for instance, both *he* and *talked* are modified by machine gun. Further classifications might include *preposition metaphors* (he had a machine gun of a mouth), *adjective metaphors* (his machine-gun mouth raked the room), and *verb metaphors*, (he machine-gunned the room with his words).

In conversation recently, I heard a *double metaphor*, parallelism created by double comparison. My friend was describing a moment when she said something that embarrassed or dazed the people in her writing workshop, "I was the headlights; they were the deer," she told me, and I felt the full impact of the moment. I was excited to have discovered a new classification of metaphor. New to me, perhaps, but I soon realized that this type of metaphor is prevalent in our conversation, in our music, in a variety of jokes and memorial speeches: I am a hydrant, you are a dog.

Finally, in *Handbook of Poetic Forms*, there's an entry for a *kenning*, where the two nouns being compared are simply juxtaposed, nothing but a hyphen between them: *gun-mouth*.

Generating Metaphor

Poems that overuse the conventions of metaphor are as tedious as poems in which an adjective has been assigned to every noun. In his *Selected Essays & Reviews*, American poet and critic Hayden Carruth writes: "For myself, I believe that metaphor generally does not work as well as direct statement, and further that the tediousness and friability of most current American

ABSTRACT NOUNS	ADJECTIVES	CONCRETE NOUNS
Truth	Careful	Snowstorm
Love	Guilty	Pile of Leaves
Fame	Blue	Angel
Necessity	Blasphemous	Junk-food Deli
Freedom	Intense	Garden

Figure 7–1. *Abstract Nouns*

poetry is owing to the overuse of metaphor more than to anything else." Among his Four Summary Admonishments on metaphor, Carruth exhorts his fellow writers: "Use metaphor sparingly and only when it accords well with all the poem's other components and is fully integrated with them. The metaphor must rise naturally from the things of the poem. Never invent a metaphor for its own sake" (1996, 225).

I agree that the best use of metaphor does "rise naturally from the things of the poem," but to help students (and myself) generate metaphor, I've recently been using an exercise Diane Swan presented at a writer's workshop I attended.

Swan asked us to make three columns of equal width. "In the first column," she instructed, "list, as quickly as possible, at least five abstract nouns. Then list at least five adjectives in the second column. Colors are okay here, but tactile adjectives are even better! In the third column, list at least five concrete nouns."

After five minutes, during which time she was busily creating her own list, Swan told us to stop writing and to look over our three columns. "If you have listed at least five items in each column, you now have at least five times five times five, 125 metaphors. Or, if you ignore the adjective column, you have at least five times five, 25 metaphors!" Adjective hater that I claim to be, I noticed with pleasure that the words in column two were often expendable. And, as Swan had implied might happen, adjectives of texture evoked stronger images than those of color.

Unmetaphor

Sometimes when a writer is stuck, it helps to turn an assignment around. "Write poorly on purpose" is an example. "Don't write a report but a play in which one of the characters delivers a speech with the information of your report" is another way to help students sneak through a blocked situation. So, for students stuck in their attempts to generate metaphor, it is sometimes helpful for them to invent *unmetaphors*, perhaps starting with any cliché that first comes to mind. "Your teeth are not like stars. . . ." Often this practice seems to demand extension, by way of explanation. Like parallel or extended metaphor, this technique may provide images or ideas worth investigating in a complete poem!

A faculty member at Vermont College scooped the following unmetaphors off the Internet, listed as the work of high school students in various essays and short stories. I would call the following entries *unmetaphors*—each for its own reason.

> The little boat gently drifted across the pond exactly the way a bowling ball wouldn't.
>
> He was as tall as a six-foot, three-inch tree.
>
> Her eyes were like two brown circles with big black dots in the center.
>
> John and Mary had never met. They were like two hummingbirds who had also never met.
>
> The thunder was ominous sounding, much like the sound of a thin sheet of metal being shaken backstage during the storm scene in a play.
>
> The red brick wall was the color of a brick-red Crayola crayon.
>
> Her vocabulary was as bad as, like, whatever.

The list also contains true metaphors, some humorous, and many of them extended.

> He spoke with the wisdom that can only come from experience, like a guy who went blind because he looked at a solar eclipse without one of those boxes with a pinhole in it and now goes around the country speaking at high schools about the dangers of looking at a solar eclipse without one of those boxes with a pinhole in it.
>
> She caught your eye like one of those pointy hook latches that used to dangle from screen doors and would fly up whenever you banged the door open again.

McBride fell twelve stories, hitting the pavement like a Hefty bag filled with vegetable soup.

The whole scene had an eerie, surreal quality, like when you're on vacation in another city and *Jeopardy* comes on at 7 P.M. instead of 7:30.

Her hair glistened in the rain like nose hair after a sneeze.

The hailstones leaped from the pavement, just like maggots when you fry them in hot grease.

Her date was pleasant enough, but she knew that if her life was a movie, this guy would be buried in the credits as something like "second tall man."

Long separated by cruel fate, the star-crossed lovers race across the grassy field toward each other like two freight trains, one having left Cleveland at 6:36 P.M. traveling at 55 mph, the other from Topeka at 4:19 P.M. at a speed of 35 mph.

The politican was unnoticed, like the period after the Dr. on a Dr Pepper can.

They lived in a typical suburban neighborhood with picket fences that resembled Nancy Kerrigan's teeth.

His thoughts tumbled in his head, making and breaking alliances like underpants in a dryer without Cling Free.

Symbolism

In that it implies comparison, *symbolism* is like metaphor. But unlike metaphor, symbolism is not always expressed verbally. Religious icons, for instance, have symbolic meanings that are conveyed without words. Likewise, a fancy automobile may be a symbol of its owner's economic success. Neither the icon nor the automobile is accompanied by words of explanation. What they stand for is in the heart or mind of the beholder. To its owner, a brand new Mercedes Benz may symbolize a successful career; to a mechanic, it may symbolize fine craftsmanship or conspicuous consumption; to a traffic officer, it may symbolize arrogance, especially if it is speeding on a foggy highway.

The interpretive nature of symbolism makes it a troublesome element in poetry. Too often, writers deflect criticism of a vague poem on the grounds of symbolism. If the success of a poem relies on the reader's getting a special symbolic meaning, the poem may register, to some readers, as little more than a riddle.

At the same time, many readers expect symbolism in every poem they read. A friend told me that my prose poem "The Sandman" (see Chapter 1), is a "religious poem" because the sandman is a symbol for God. I was surprised, amused, and honored: His assertion was certainly news to me.

My friend's unintended flattery illustrates why I don't trust symbolism. Having been over-subjected to teachers who find a hidden symbol in practically every line of poetry, readers often make absurd conjectures, losing sight of a poem's literal intent. And, when it is used intentionally, symbolism rarely works as a device without being so overt that the poem seems bloated.

Used less obviously, symbolism offers false comfort to the author that the work has special significance —at least for the discerning reader. This attitude may serve some writers well, but it usually leads to reader alienation.

If symbolism is permitted to emerge from a writer's or reader's unconscious associations and the connections that are made among the images of a poem, *and is not the point of that writing*, its presence will enrich the reader's experience and give unique significance to that poem. Acknowledging this very personalness or uniqueness, the reader who fails to make symbolic connections is fully entitled to say, "I don't get it." And this, I think, is where the discussion of any given poem should start: What is it trying to do?

Traditionally, the privilege of saying "I don't get it" has been reserved for the teacher, responding to *the students'* poems. The teacher has always understood the poems in the textbook, with their three levels of meaning, one of which is symbolic; for on his lap—under the desk or out of sight— lies the magic key to all understanding: a *Teacher's Guide*. At least during my junior high and high school days, essays and tests were graded largely on the basis of one's agreement with the magic key; poetry rarely offered opportunity for speculation or personal interpretation. One listened to the lecture and parroted what was heard.

Deep Image Poems

During the 1970s, a group of prominent U.S. poets were labeled as the "deep-image school." They wrote deep-image poems that, more than anything, were characterized by their reliance on visual imagery, usually through series of metaphors or similes. The poems did not have any musical tradition in common. They were neither metrical nor rhymed, and they did not seek to tell a story. Their sparse, declarative mood served to let the deep-image bones of the poem speak for themselves. Here is one such poem, by Philip Dow.

Early Morning

The solitary egret
in a field of new barley.

I think of the loneliness
of angels—lacking even
the body of a shadow
to share.

The immediacy of such a poem calls to mind the haiku. The statement the poem makes is the unspoken half of the equation between poem and reader. This implies a lot of trust (or, conceivably, indifference) from the author. "What I think isn't what matters," a deep-image poet might rationalize. "I just put out the images and let readers make of them what they may." This is the equivalent of relying on symbolism. The reader's ability to make associations, to deduce conscious equivalents, determines whether the poem succeeds.

It all boils down to the poet's intent: Does the symbolism or metaphor explain the unexplainable, provide fresh insight, or evoke an emotional or visceral response? If not, I argue, it must have such strong personal meaning that it acts as a bookmark to the author, without distracting the reader.

Exercises

1. From demands to prayers: the imperative mood. Create a series of demands, possibly in a sequence that moves from adamant to prayerful. Can this list be revised into a poem?

2. Write a poem that addresses an important social issue or that tells a story.

3. Write a poem that Martha Washington might have written for George on the eve of his inauguration.

4. Write a poem that incorporates two or three principles of biology or mathematics. Or write a poem that investigates some of the notions of science fiction.

5. Write a poem for two voices. (Anyone who is stuck might consider

using a simple question and answer format, possibly basing the poem on an actual interview.)

6. Take a well-known advertising phrase and build a poem around it, possibly repeating the key phrase at strategic moments in the poem.

Disposable

I guess that once the crippled crud impales the
mouth
of my tube of toothpaste
I buy another

Or when my toothbrush itself is tarnished
with a yellow tint
and each bristle is contorted into knots
I buy another

Kind of like when the razor rust
runs down my leg
and slashes it in half
I buy another

Or my gallon of skim milk separates
and tastes like the way
a dog smells
I buy another

Or when my radio static
empowers the world
I buy another

Now nothing is made to last
Everything is disposable

▼

The strength in this poem is the overexaggeration of situations. For
example, the razor rust cannot possibly cut a leg in half. The poem
also conveys a message about recycling and society. The words are
chosen carefully, and the line breaks are very natural. However, I am
not sure if the iteration of "I buy another" works. I like the way repetition sounds in other people's poems, especially when they are
read out loud. However, I am not sure if I can make it sound right.
I have repeated the lines so many times I feel immune to their
meaning and rhythm.

—*Claire Feldman*

8

The Poems of Others

Assessing and Responding to Student Poems

Assessment

The more external the source, the less useful the assessment to the poet. The teacher's comments are not as important as the opinions of one's peers, and, finally, the poet's own judgments are what matters. What this suggests is a poetry curriculum that involves the development of classroom consensus on what matters in a good poem, and the gradual shifting of judgment from the teacher to the students and, ultimately, to the author. With young writers and with some middle school students, it's important to explain that the *subject* of the poem is not considered in the assessment. Otherwise, responses often fall into the "I like it because it's about horses" category, relatively useless information for the author.

Well, what does matter in a poem?

- Visual appearance or aural impact
- Conveyance of feeling or ideas
- Clarity
- Use of evocative language (sensory images or metaphors, rhythmic or musical word choice)

Given that many poets use a variety of strategies to supplant the conventions of grammar, usage, and mechanics, poetry may provide the ultimate opportunity to teach "the rules." If the poet were to present this poem as a prose essay, how would it be punctuated? In what ways would you edit the apparent sentence fragments, how would you revise the run-on sentences, and what other changes would be necessary to turn this poem into conventional prose?

Expecting unresolvable discussions about grammar, usage, and mechanics in poetry, I would establish criteria for poetry assessment that considered, not correctness, but *consistency*. "If it's consistent, the author may break the rules with impunity," I would say. "Of course, we'll ask you to explain which rules you've broken, and why." In the same way that Claire Feldman has annotated her poems with critical comment, students might add to their portfolios some commentary on the rules they have intentionally broken.

With any engaged group of young people, a skilled teacher can ask the question: "What is it that you like to find in the poems you read?" The brainstormed responses to this question become the criteria by which the students assess their own, and each other's, poems. Listing a dozen or more such criteria, some of them perhaps contradictory of each other, implies a myriad of strategies from which each poet can choose one or more goals for each poem. An author's completed portfolio of poems might, in some way, have covered the entire list of criteria!

Defining Response

As I mentioned earlier, Dave Smith advises teachers to avoid referring to the author in responding to a student's writing, instead talking about the narrator. Instead of, "What are *you* trying to convey here?" he recommends asking, "What is *the narrator* trying to convey here?" This is an important stance, allowing the author plenty of wiggle room to accept praise and criticism alike, and it provides psychic space to explore a range of emotions, circumstances, and "weird" imagery. On any given day, I can create a narrator who shows emotions or tells stories that may or may not be *my* emotions or stories! Whether or not student Erin Miksic is assuming a persona in "Diseased," I would respond to *the narrator's* words, not the words of Erin Miksic.

> Joyous and full of life in spring
> In fall only to you I cling
>
> In winter I huddle terribly close
> I am as free in summer as a ghost

I wish I were independently stable
and not like an emotional cable

I want to be more self-reliant
and not a little girl so pale and pliant

To lose this severe addiction
would rid my soul of this affliction

My first instinct, reading this poem, is to mention the image created by "emotional cable." I can acknowledge my admiration of these words, and draw attention to the fact that they, alone, play to my bias in favor of the concrete image. Is there a reason to have this poem rhyme? Does the rhyme create a situation where some of the sentences sound unnatural? If so, is this intentional? Is the narrator's use of this form a way of conveying a specific attitude or level of development?

What is the effect of starting the poem with a one-and-a-half line adjectival phrase? Would a *scene* better portray the level of dependency expressed in the poem? Might a second scene provide the contrasting freedom of summer and spring? Why are the seasons presented nonchronologically?

Are there concrete, physical details or sets of details that would give the reader a visual equivalent to the three abstract nouns in the final stanza?

It might overwhelm a poet to have all these questions posed at the same time, but one or two of them, during a brief conversation, might help the writer to refocus the poem or write a new poem with a broader set of strategies.

Too much praise often stifles students. So, instead of praise, I believe in encouragement and challenge, discussion of the alternatives the narrator may have considered—using revision as an opportunity to engage young writers in the practical application of specific skills, reminding them, at all times, that revision doesn't always result in improvement!

Response Without Evaluation

Sometimes it's useful to ask everyone in the class to attempt the same kind of revision. Perhaps without having read any of the poems, and in a way that is arbitrary and judgment free, I suggest that the students narrow the focus, introduce dialogue, cut half the adjectives and choose more precise nouns, or rewrite the whole poem in the second person, present tense. In this way, the students are challenged to see their poems anew, *to consider alternatives*.

The poem that's being revised will probably not improve as much as future efforts, which will gradually reflect an increased awareness of the alternatives that have been explored. Quietly recognizing such improvements in fresh poems, the teacher can steer a young writer along a highly individual path, simply specifying choices and a variety of strategies for each assignment. Key each assignment to one or more of your curriculum goals and develop strategies of response that encourage each student to recognize and develop areas of interest and strength.

Response with Evaluation

In yesterday's classrooms, evaluation was pretty much the only response a student could get. The poem may or may not have actually received a grade, and the gist of a teacher's comments was subjective response: "I like this metaphor" (often accompanied by a smiley face); "Watch your spelling!" "This makes me sad" (though it was a rare teacher who acknowledged feelings!); "I can *see* this scene!"

Now, thanks to the teachings of Donald Graves and many writers and teachers after him, we more easily let go of subjective judgments in favor of open-ended questions whose goal is to nudge the student into uncharted waters. At its most basic level, this type of response is driven by evaluation, but the teacher's responses are neutral, devoid of judgment. "Could this scene, visual as it is, be expressed through dialogue or action? Maybe not in this poem, but can you write a piece, maybe on a brand new topic, that uses dialogue or physical action to help paint the scene?"

One might look at a student's third or fourth attempt at dialogue and acknowledge that the author has mastered the open and end quotes, as well as the elements of correct English. "Now, I wonder if you can listen to some conversations over lunch today and notice patterns of declarative and interrogative and exclamatory speech, the numbers of incomplete sentences. Can you write a poem with dialogue in the style of what you hear in the cafeteria?"

These kinds of suggestions can emanate from all-group discussions, individual conferences, or the usual "writers' workshop" atmosphere, where everyone is invited to offer comments. In these settings, participants often preface their remarks, "I like it, but . . ." which is a pretty bald way of trying to mask the judgment already implied in the first two words. I don't suppose these judgments do much harm, as long as everyone agrees that they are human and therefore fallible responses, and as long as we recognize that the author is the true judge. It's just that time is usually wasted by "I like," "I don't like" comments, because what an author really needs to know is:

> Did the reader receive the message or feeling I intended?
>
> Did my message/feeling have any effect on the reader?
>
> What can I do differently, in this or in future poems?

As various school districts develop standards for English Language Arts and other disciplines, teachers recognize the value of a common vocabulary. Various writing assessment programs, including Vermont's statewide program, with which I've been working since 1989, develop and publish writing rubrics that offer graphic representation of commonly accepted criteria. By representing and scoring each criterion independently, providing an array of scores (not just an averaged-out number), a program can convey the importance of each component of successful writing. At statewide or districtwide levels, program rubrics are, nevertheless, likely to be fairly general.

Remembering the importance of local ownership of standards, one can surely envision a classroom where students generate their own rubric, possibly altering it as their skills develop. Donald Graves has pointed out that students who brainstorm their own sets of standards are not likely to stray too far from whatever some distant, districtwide committee has devised. Further, learning to apply their own criteria to their writing prepares students to apply the standards of a broader community. Students can achieve a critical sense of ownership and understanding of the standards when they are encouraged to articulate and strive for what they value.

Of course, if evaluations are being made, it's also a matter of fairness that whoever is being evaluated be told the standards of evaluation before submitting whatever it is that is to be judged. This is knowing the rules before the game starts, a relatively new concept in education. I knew that my typed papers could contain no mispellings or strikeovers, but Mr. Chancellor never bothered to tell his students the other secrets to getting an A, so all I knew was that "The Tears of Separation" (see Chapter 1), because it was "Out-Shelleying Shelley," deserved only a C–. If Mr. Chancellor had explained that flowery language and melodramatic themes would receive lower grades than spontaneous and clear expressions of joy, I might have written a poem more to his liking. And, alas, in those days, it was the teacher's liking for which I was writing!

Mr. Chancellor might have asked me about the process of writing such a poem and whether I had enjoyed that process. In what ways might my future poems be different from this one? His questions could have led me from my recently completed work to poems I hadn't yet thought of writing.

Instead, he was a pretentious man who harbored secret biases.

Bias

Bias often connotes prejudice. I prefer to see it as idiosyncratic preference. Acknowledging bias is an important first step in coming to agreement on standards. Maybe we can all agree that poems should convey information or a feeling, but how do I deal with the fact that I don't like poems about dinosaurs? My bias doesn't gibe with defensible standards; that's what makes it a bias. If this bias is strong enough, I owe it to myself and to my students to acknowledge it, one of the bugs in my brain-mounted poetry evaluation program. The user of my program simply needs to know how to avoid triggering that bug.

By acknowledging my own biases (unnecessary adjectives and adverbs, excessive use of participles; *i*'s and *j*'s dotted with circles or hearts; blood and gore poems), I pave the way for students to consider and articulate their own. Further, once students see that I have bias, my judgments are likely to be seen as coming from a human, and therefore fallible, source. Call it step one in the quest to have student poets become their own best critics!

Positive Bias

In a discussion of bias, it will certainly be helpful to acknowledge what it is that, perhaps unreasonably, we *do* like. I like the idea of the poem as a novel, or at least a sort of story or screenplay. Occasionally I'm awed by a short lyric, but maybe because I'm happier when a good long poem seems to be rolling from my careening inkball than when I'm crafting the perfect six to ten lines, I prefer poems that reveal a personality, the narrator or storyteller. I like poems that evoke more than one feeling. I like poems that use plain, everyday language. I like poems with precise nouns and verbs.

I think of it as a bias, but it's a tenet of good writing: Good writing doesn't describe an emotion, it creates scenes and images that impart emotion. Rare lyrics, lucky hits, impart their emotion in the fewest lines. It's easier to win a reader with something a little longer, a little airier.

Again, asking students to discuss their positive biases will increase everyone's awareness of strategies that lead to appreciative readers. In every case, I have found that acknowledging my biases at the beginning of a course, and announcing new biases as they occur to me throughout my work with a group, helps me to offer whatever subjective evaluation I feel compelled to offer without appearing unduly authoritarian. Because it's a bias, the students can consider its validity in light of their own, personal standards! The conversations that result from conflicting standards are at the heart of both missionary and contemplative writing. Is this what we mean by poetic spirit?

Holy

Holy as a dreamed up angel
I look like a swine from . . .
!Gotch Ya Joker!
the truth is people hide secrets in their shoes.
shoeless you are. got no secrets.
deep ones that dismantle a heart? . . .
Holy heartless bastard you've got no shoes!
I heard you hit it off with a rugby player from downtown.
she smiles like crest toothpaste has taken her empty hours.
the wind brushes her hair.
unlike you and me
the wind snarls it up into a nest.
a nest darling
that's what I said
A bird house where baby is born . . .
born bad can't fly broken wing . . .
yeah I broke one of these once.
riding a horse fell to the ground
childhood cries out like a bit of a radio show
can't wait for the next commercial
but you call it that if it's only words?
Answer me lonely rugby player
I see your shoes
hiding something darling?

▼

This poem is the product of a freewrite. This rushed style of writing usually does not produce poetry that I slightly consider to renovate, though there are always exceptions. The flavor of this poem creates a character and a defined attitude. Here the line breaks are of hardly any importance, while the punctuation exploits the feeling of the narrator. When I read this poem it tends to remind me of a monologue that is taken in one breath. If this were included in a script, the most important stage direction would indicate that the reader must speak this excerpt as fast as possible. Basically, the poem is the ravings of a madwoman. The use of shoes and secrets is a simple theme. I have tried to tinker with this poem to see how it could be improved, though I constantly refer back to the first draft. I think this is because the word choices solely create the character of the narrator.

—*Claire Feldman*

9

Writing for Performance, Writing to Publish

Establishing specific plans for public performances inspires many writers to create new work. Some ideas will originate with the vision of the performance itself, not from the object on a page that is a stodgy, old poem! And, of course, at some point, the author will need to put on paper exactly what is planned to happen on stage—the script. And here is where it becomes a stodgy, old poem! Students who might never have agreed to try a poem in this mode will gladly create a performance that incorporates a chant, uses more than one voice, requires movement, or otherwise calls forth performance skills.

Certainly, by the time they reach middle school age, students are ready to go beyond the traditional "author's tea," where student after student rushes to the podium and blurts a poem. Let's consider the possibility of regular performances, where only a few students at a time present their work—the regularity and brevity of these occasions helping to build audience, performance by performance.

Such performances can be incorporated into other planned events, perhaps serving as warm-up acts for school assemblies or evening productions. They can be featured before sports events or maybe over the school's intercom right after the Pledge of Allegiance. Indeed, they can be presented in local libraries, in visits to retirement homes, at PTA meetings—anywhere and anytime the teacher thinks ears and hearts can be reached. Think of the power of a single student proudly reading a recent poem to start a school board meeting!

Promoting these events through the local newspaper and school newsletters will help attract an audience. A regular feature in the local paper might announce forthcoming events and, at the same time, publish student writing. But even more effective in attracting audience is the word of mouth that dynamic performances can generate.

How to make these performances dynamic? Brevity and attitude are key here! Limiting such events to fifteen minutes, tops, will ensure that no one grows bored. Consider organizing these minievents around a common theme or attitude. Suggest a mode of presentation to help the students select appropriate poems and deliver those poems in a coherent fashion and format.

The most effective group poetry presentation I've seen was orchestrated by poet Verandah Porche. She'd been given fifteen minutes of stage time for a group of fourteen high school poets. Rather than lose time as each poet made an entrance, Porche had the entire group on stage throughout the fifteen minutes. During the applause at the conclusion of each poem, the group would briefly churn, absorbing the poet who was being applauded as a new reader emerged from the group to approach the microphone. The group would then freeze, focusing attention on the performer at the microphone. All fourteen students read their poems in less than fifteen minutes, and the readings were not rushed! No time was lost between poems, and every student, knowing that "statue stillness" and "riveted attention" on each reader were crucial to success, gained a full fifteen minutes of stage experience.

When I mention attitude, I mean physical positioning and the unifying *emotional* attitude of the event. Think of this as theatre, a short play, and present it with the same care given to the production of a one-act play, even though it requires nowhere near as much group rehearsal. Each student can rehearse at home, with two whole-group rehearsals the week of the actual presentation. At these rehearsals the teacher can focus on the speaking skills of each student and the whole group's execution of format.

What other options are likely to shape or suggest attitude? Simple costuming requirements (e.g., everyone wears jeans and a dark shirt) will enhance the focus of dress rehearsals and, of course, the performance. Setting—even an imagined setting—will contribute to attitude. The students can re-create a beatniks' cafe reading or a hippies' convention, or a formal, classical approach, as in a traditional reading. They can videotape their production, or present a talent-show format where readings are interspersed with musical or other theatrical presentations. And, requiring considerably more group rehearsal, poems can be performed as choral recitations or staged plays.

The Poetry Slam

This recent cultural phenomenon blends all the qualities of traditional and beatnik/hippie readings, adding a good measure of "Gong Show" irreverence. Although I have never attended one, my understanding is that the rules and format of a *slam* depend on the emcee's mood or on local tradition. Surely some enterprising group of junior or senior high student poets could devise an official guidebook, complete with photographs and sample poems, a documented slam in development, then carry that model on to their respective colleges and careers.

A slam is, most surely, a performance/competition where, I'm told, the audience votes on the best poem/performance. Heckling and yowling are not discouraged, so slams can create whole new attitudes toward poetry.

Poetry Marathons

In the summer of 1983, Janet Ressler and poets Steve Ward, Gary Moore, and Nadell Fishman initiated a Vermontwide celebration of poetry, an eight-hour outdoor gathering—followed by a street dance—where more than a hundred Vermont writers gathered in Montpelier, on the State House Lawn, to read their poems. The marathon was unjuried, but each poet had to register at least two weeks before the event, agreeing to abide by the schedule that would be established in response to the number of registrants.

It turned out that each poet was allowed five minutes at the microphone. An excellent sound system (and the poets' respect for the time limit) contributed to a relaxing day. Audience members could come and go as they pleased, listening intently or drinking slurpies and playing frisbee on the fringes. The size of the audience, throughout the day, varied from twenty or thirty people to more than three hundred. Lapel buttons were presented to each of the poets who had volunteered to read: I ran at the mouth: Vermont Poetry Marathon: Montpelier, VT, August 3, 1983.

Poetry Potluck Poker

One of my favorite ways to structure a poetry reading combines the best features of a reading and a workshop. Like a potluck supper, everyone is invited to bring a creation. And, like a poker game, each participant may pass or throw something into the pot. I set the chairs up in a circle, and we simply start with someone who seems eager to read a poem, then proceed around the circle with each participant given the opportunity to accept or decline as many as three to five minutes in the spotlight. Depending on how many participants choose to read their work, second and third rounds are sometimes possible. But, just to be sure that no one is left out in case there's no time for a second round, I discourage sandbagging, where one passes in the first round, then jumps in during round two.

Reading Poems Aloud/Performing Them

Have you ever been burned by a bad poetry reading, a performance that went on too long in a room that was poorly ventilated or too big for the event?

Invited to a small college in North Carolina to read my poems, I was met at the airport by the student organizer, who rushed me to the campus, directly into the fine arts center and onto a giant stage with a podium, pitcher of water, and microphone all waiting. The curtain was closed but I could hear her on the apron of the stage, lifting the microphone from its stand and embarking on a vigorous reading of my résumé, then setting the mike down and rushing offstage to draw the curtains. "Without further ado . . ." mike rumbling . . . patter of feet: "Here's Geof Hewitt!" shouted from offstage, and the curtains squealing apart before my eyes to reveal my audience . . . four students and a teacher, sitting together, third row center, soon joined by the student organizer.

Thinking fast, I asked if we might move to a more intimate setting, and learned that the mortuary in the college chapel was the only other available space. "Fine," I replied, and we proceeded across campus to that mahogany and stained glass room where, amid fresh-cut lilacs, I read my poems and benefited from the informal comments and questions of the teacher and students.

As much as anything, good performances rely on an appropriate space and an awareness of the performer-audience tension that can be exacerbated or defused by the appropriate choice of venue, by the pacing of the performance, and by a careful (lucky?) balance of planning and spontaneity. Does one want a formal or easygoing mood for the event? As far as breaking the ice between an audience and the performance, it's always a great idea to start off with something humorous.

The Pause

When novice readers hit the stage, their first impulse is usually to double the speed of everything. Practice and concentration can help students overcome this natural tendency. Equally important, in any dramatic presentation, is the pause! A drama coach once explained to me the importance of gathering and focusing an audience's energy. At its simplest, this means simply using a long pause before starting a presentation, allowing the audience to settle, and then some. The same technique, for dramatic effect, can be used *within* the performance.

I was working on performance skills with a group of sixth-grade students recently, coaching a girl (who was obviously up to the challenge) to read her poem more slowly. She seemed enthusiastic, so I had her read the poem three times. After the third reading I could sense that she'd had enough, even if she'd only slowed the pace by a hair. "Okay," I said. "Tomorrow, I'm going to want you not only to read even slower than that, but to pause, good and long, somewhere, just to build audience tension." She smiled, a little relieved that this little session was, at last, over.

The next day I asked her to read her new poem. "Remember to read slowly, and don't forget to pause somewhere—long enough to create a really dramatic effect!"

She read slowly and with confidence, and the poem was pretty good. "I could hear every word," I complimented her after a few moments of silence, "but I didn't hear much of a pause."

"Mr. Hewitt," she replied patiently, "I'm not through!"

To help writers find the correct performance elements for their readings, have them exchange poems and critique or direct one another's readings. And have them rehearse the poems they *have* written. This works best when the critique involves active coaching, ongoing theatre direction, rather than director's notes at the end of the rehearsal.

Publishing: Maybe This Is a Local Event

Of course, *to publish* means, simply, to make public. So any public performance or exhibition of a poem means, in the formal sense, that it has been published. Often, however, a writer wants a larger group of readers than that assembled at a public performance or exhibit.

Self-publishing is the most common form of student publishing. A one-sheet format is the simplest way to accomplish this, yielding as many as eight usable pages (see Figure 9–1). Making little books this way helps a writer develop an awareness of design, including type font and page layout, and production techniques. Most self-published writers master the complexities of production, but find that *distribution* is another matter. Keep the press run small, say 100 copies, and resolve to save half for posterity.

The local newspaper and school publications are other avenues for young poets and their teachers. As with poetry performances, the poem is often best received where or when it is least expected. Literary magazines are often too crowded for poems to have necessary breathing space. An alternative to sardinelike publication is to place just one or two poems in each school board report, in the school's Annual Report, and in classroom newsletters. Such opportunities for publication might become part of a school's tradition.

But some young authors (or their parents or teachers) are hungry for wider recognition and submit poems to national publications and competitions. So many poets in the United States are lusting for publication that a vanity-driven industry has sprung up to provide whole anthologies that are endowed with flowery titles, on sale at ridiculously inflated prices, purchased usually only by the very people who contributed the poems therein. I was first published in one such anthology, in 1962. I paid $6.95 (big money then!) for a paperback anthology (entitled *Young Voices*), tiny type mimeographed on 8½ x 11-inch copy paper, my seven-line poem (the shortest I had submitted) sandwiched among the short poems of 250 other young writers. It didn't take but a minute, on opening the anthology, to realize that I'd been had.

Do not pay to have poems published! Do not agree to publish poems where you are required to purchase the publication as a condition of participation. Do not agree to attend award ceremonies that charge the awardees a fee to attend the banquet.

With only the rarest of exceptions, the road to legitimate publishing, especially where poetry is concerned, is time-consuming, discouraging, and definitely not cost effective. The very few publications that actually pay more than a few dollars for poetry are so competitive that they typically receive 300–400 poems for every one they have space to print. On the other hand, more than a thousand poetry markets exist where the editors offer a modest fee or contributor's copies of the publication, and a few of these are publications with a specific interest in poems by young people. In the Bibliography, I list *The 21st Century*, which is written entirely by teenagers, and *Potato Hill Poetry, Merlyn's Pen,* and *English Journal,* which are receptive to the work of students *and* teachers!

Although my first experience in publishing was disheartening, I continued sending my work out regularly, and by the time I reached college I was regularly submitting my poems to about a dozen little and national magazines. I had no luck, year after year. Determined to be "discovered," even if I had to be the discoverer, I took a course in book design. This gave me access to a print shop and, during my senior year, I self-published my first collection of poems, a chapbook. I loved the process of setting the type and hand-feeding the flatbed press! Shortly thereafter, one of my poems was accepted by a legitimate little magazine, which sent me two contributor's copies as payment.

A year or two thereafter, as a graduate student, I began to encounter less resistance, and my ratio of poems submitted to poems accepted for publication fell from something like 200 to 1 to approximately 40 to 1. It didn't matter that no one but a few fellow-writers knew of the magazines that were accepting my work, I was getting *published!*

But the thrill disappears as fast as it takes to read the publication that bears one's work. Oh sure, show it around, but there's a limit to how many people you want to show your published poem to. And there's even a smaller number of people that one knows who will come upon the poem otherwise. Short of publishing a whole book, the writer of a poem that appears in a little or national magazine *rarely* hears a thing from readers. *Organic Gardening*, with a circulation in excess of one million readers, published a poem of mine in the 1970s. I can recall two or three comments from friends, dedicated gardeners, who happened to stumble upon my poem. A few years later I published three or four poems in the local newspaper, with its circulation of approximately 10,000 readers. In response to that publication, I received postcards, phone calls, and eight or ten comments from neighbors at the local store.

The more local the publication, the more likely that one will receive confirmation from one's readers. Unless, that is, you're such a good poet or by some twist of fate become so famous that you attract the level of attention that is focused on our very few poetry stars. Maybe I can name 200 if I really strain my mind. The rest of us, and I'll spare you a list of names, occasionally publish poems in magazines or in anthologies or in whole collections. Whether a star or a lesser-known writer, most poets are more thrilled by the experience of *writing* the poem than by publication or any flurry of response (unlikely as it is) to that publication. In the late 1960s, *kayak* magazine quoted Margaret Atwood on the value of publishing: "It makes your work fireproof."

I have always been fascinated by the variety of styles of self-publication devised by imaginative young people. For some, the poem is an object, displayed and perhaps titled as sculpture might be displayed and titled: "Poem Written on Orange Peel that has Dried and Hardened." For others, it's a mass-produced photocopied book made from a single sheet of $8\frac{1}{2}$ x 11-inch

HOMEMADE BOOKS

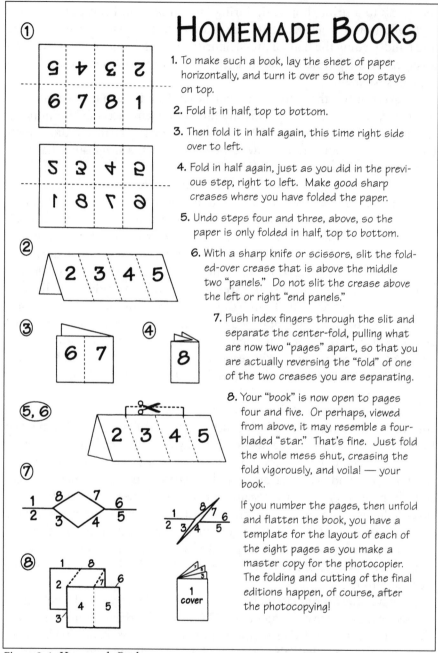

1. To make such a book, lay the sheet of paper horizontally, and turn it over so the top stays on top.

2. Fold it in half, top to bottom.

3. Then fold it in half again, this time right side over to left.

4. Fold in half again, just as you did in the previous step, right to left. Make good sharp creases where you have folded the paper.

5. Undo steps four and three, above, so the paper is only folded in half, top to bottom.

6. With a sharp knife or scissors, slit the folded-over crease that is above the middle two "panels." Do not slit the crease above the left or right "end panels."

7. Push index fingers through the slit and separate the center-fold, pulling what are now two "pages" apart, so that you are actually reversing the "fold" of one of the two creases you are separating.

8. Your "book" is now open to pages four and five. Or perhaps, viewed from above, it may resemble a four-bladed "star." That's fine. Just fold the whole mess shut, creasing the fold vigorously, and voila! — your book.

If you number the pages, then unfold and flatten the book, you have a template for the layout of each of the eight pages as you make a master copy for the photocopier. The folding and cutting of the final editions happen, of course, after the photocopying!

Figure 9–1. *Homemade Books*

paper, printed on just one side, specially folded and cut to yield, without staples, an eight-page, pocket-sized booklet.

Some self-publishing writers make limited editions of their work, gathering pages of carefully selected papers, sewn by a shoelace. Whatever the format and style of publication, it says that the writer cares about the work, and it is an invitation, to any audience it attracts, into that writer's mind and heart. It is an expression of trust, second only to a handwritten letter.

Risque

with a rip rap in my abdomen
a newspaper in hand
the head
line:
Suffix of suffering
a boy in a frock . . .
with no smock,
to cover his
cleavage

dress shoes
earrings
sports team tackle club
is not for all those kids,
neither
is a boy in a dress

what a(n)
a(dis)traction
for that black tie school
to settle
for less
than a
(law)
suit

▼

This poem is based on a single incident at Burlington High School, where a boy was expelled for wearing a dress to school. It is very difficult to tell if a reader without this knowledge would fully understand the poem. The first verse is a synopsis of the event. There is a bit of a rhyming scheme and the line breaks almost convey a visual image of a woman, although that was not entirely intentional. The second verse is a commentary on my own beliefs without flat-out saying "I think." This part is not quite as clear as the first verse. The last verse is a play on words, staging the situation as a pun. First, black tie and law suit remind one of a lawyer, plus a dress suit, which is composed of pant and a tie. Also, the parentheses in "a(n)" display perfect grammar for a "perfect school." The other parentheses help convey the puns with less confusion.

—*Claire Feldman*

10
Portfolios and the Poetry-centered Classroom

Keeping a portfolio of one's poems is an important learning tool. One step short of publication, a portfolio gathers the work a writer most values, and provides a history of development over weeks, months, or a lifetime.

The strategies for keeping a portfolio are as varied as the personalities and preferences of people who keep portfolios. As an expression of individuality, a portfolio reflects in format of presentation, as well as in its contents, the spirit of its creator. And because a portfolio *should* be an expression of individuality, organizational rules and guidelines, I believe, should be kept to a minimum.

In *A Portfolio Primer: Teaching, Collecting, and Assessing Student Writing* (Heinemann 1995), I explore the all-important issue of *ownership*. As with single pieces of writing, the more control the author retains over the portfolio (including its format, what goes into it, where it is kept, and all other matters of responsibility), the more likely it is that the author will value the portfolio. To the degree that programs impose uniformity on the portfolio, they diminish author ownership and thus, predictably, the author's enthusiasm for the portfolio.

A poetry portfolio may range from a thin, careful selection of finished drafts of original work to a bulging scrapbook of drafts and finished copies of original work and favorite poems by other authors. Students who are really excited about poetry may wind up with two portfolios: one stuffed with working drafts and just about everything else, and one that is a careful selection of finished work.

In the same way that Claire Feldman annotates the poems that introduce each chapter of this book, students often enjoy leading a partner through the poetry portfolio and reflecting on each poem, describing how and why it was written, explaining their processes and aesthetic responses.

Poetry Across the Curriculum

If poetry writing is seen as a tool for exploring attitudes, its relevance to all curricula becomes obvious; it offers, at the least, an opportunity to express frustration or anger for the student who resents having to take a course. It opens a fresh line of communication between student and instructor. It provides a connection between the verbal learning within a classroom and the imaginative world that makes learning memorable.

While the ideal classroom might provide integration of *all* the arts, let's be realistic and hope to build an interarts curriculum that takes advantage of each teacher's artistic interests, strengths, and obsessions. A math teacher who loves painting should feel professionally obligated to integrate that love with the love of mathematics. Same goes for the teacher who's a movie fan, an actor, painter, or drummer. As always, this requires less teacher expertise than curiosity and enthusiasm. Teachers who write with their students know that the teacher who explores the artistic discipline is almost always more effective than the one who lectures. Young people need to see engagement in learning, not feel that they are the targets of teaching! In many ways, the more naïve the teacher, the bigger the lesson: Modeling the curiosity and effort of an engaged beginner is a powerful way to help students learn to learn!

Take dance. Like music, like painting or any of the graphic arts, it seems a natural for mathematics. Space and velocity, as well as simpler concepts, are major elements in dance, which demands mathematical calculation or at least some thoughtful estimation.

Where, in the masterpieces, and in your personal favorites, are the concepts of your discipline most evident and how can your students experience that correlation without your having to say too much about it? Can *they* find and articulate the correlation, learning to find in unlikely places the link between pleasure (the art) and research (the subject)? On the most basic level, a history course might include a unit on the poetry of the historic period, with students challenged to write poems in a similar vein. In the sciences, lab reports can be presented as poems and assuming the persona of a pioneer can lead to the imaginative extension that is crucial to scientific discovery.

Key to creating a poetry-centered curriculum is ensuring that the resulting work is celebrated in a variety of ways. Poetry readings within the school and at local libraries and coffeehouses (see Chapter 9) provide one form of such celebration. Displays of poems in the hallways, using a variety of graphic strategies, from embroidered quilts to banners to typed manuscripts matted or framed, can inspire schoolwide attention to ways language can be displayed like paintings.

A Flexible Curriculum: Beware Anything That's Neatly Outlined!

Keeping in mind the desirability of creating audience, I have outlined a progressive series of poetry celebrations within the following curriculum. Kept simple and well-promoted, these events can take on a life of their own; a monthly coffeehouse, for instance, may generate wide interest and become part of a school's tradition which, in turn, inspires more and more student writing. Suggest to your most interested students that they schedule three such coffeehouses and that they then decide, after watching attendance figures and feeling the "buzz" among their peers and teachers, whether they will continue to take responsibility for promotion, setup, and cleanup of a regularly scheduled, monthly (or weekly?) coffeehouse.

Let me also mention my misgivings about prefabricated curricula. To the extent that they suggest activities and approaches, they can be useful. Their relationship to actual classroom time, however, is so individual that it seems folly to present a model curriculum in time-allocated segments. Any recommended activity in the following outline might be the focus of an entire semester, or might be covered (a loaded word!) in less time than the recommended minimum two hours. Similarly, the sequence of activities is flexible: Make it your own! Blend it into the natural rhythms of your classrooms. And stay mindful of Donald Graves' exhortation: "The real curriculum is *what happened*, and we don't pay enough attention to that!"

In other words, think about the day just passed—what worked? How can tomorrow's classroom build on what was most successful today?

Thirty Weeks of Fun with Words
Week 1. Experiencing Short Poems

a) Each student writes a definition of poetry.

b) Each student writes a short poem that fits that definition.

c) Students volunteer to read their definitions (discussion) and the poems that exemplify those definitions (discussion).

d) Students write short poems that contradict their definitions.

e) Read and discuss.

f) Distribute collections of at least twenty short, short poems (see Bibliography). Students read silently, skimming for favorites. Then ask students to read their favorites aloud.

g) Discuss the reader's voice and the poet's voice. How are they different?

Homework: Find more work by the poet(s) whose short poems you most admire, and bring some of that work to class.

Week 2. Short Poems and Public Reading

a) Students read to each other the poems they've found for homework. Discussion after each reading addresses the voice and attitude of the reader and of the author.

b) The components of successful public reading (see Chapter 9).

c) Spend at least fifteen minutes leading a discussion of approaches students might take in writing their own short poems in the style or voice of their chosen poets.

d) In no more than ten minutes of fast writing, participants generate their own poems.

e) Reading and discussion of poems from D, above.

Homework: Students revise or expand their new poems; this is not an exercise in recopying, but in making revisions on their existing manuscripts. "Bring photocopies or an overhead of those marked-up manuscripts to next week's class!"

Week 3. Revision

a) Students lead discussions of the copies or overhead projection of their marked-up manuscripts. "The changes I made and why I made them."

b) Parts of Speech Revision (see Chapter 3). Students prepare fresh copies of their short poem-in-progress and conduct a word-by-word analysis organized by parts of speech, first considering alternatives for each verb, then for each noun, and so on, until alternative words have been considered for every word in the poem.

Homework: Continue parts of speech revision of short poem-in-progress or write a new short poem and bring it in with parts of speech revision markings. Consider an early draft and the final draft of these poems for the portfolio.

Week 4. Generating Topics

a) Reading and discussion of the parts of speech–revised short poems.

b) Generating Topics: Prepare a series of headings before class, write one on the board and have the students brainstorm specific topics for it; list responses on the board, then move to a new heading. Consider such headings as: An object of great beauty; Disappointing situations; Moments of great surprise; Rituals—religious and otherwise; Something I hate; Something I love; Something I've always wondered about; Something I know a lot about.

Homework: Select a topic from the brainstormed list on the board and write a poem over the weekend.

Week 5. Attitude and Point of View

a) Read and discuss the poems written for homework.

b) Discuss attitude and point of view. Brainstorm the variety of attitudes a poem might convey. What are the strategies a writer uses to convey a specific attitude?

c) Revise homework poems or write new ones that convey strong attitude.

d) Read and discuss.

Homework: Read short poems again, looking for one(s) heavy with attitude.

Week 6. First Poetry Celebration

a) Read and discuss short poems selected from last week's homework assignment. How does the reader's style of presentation emphasize or temper the poems' attitudes?

b) Plan first poetry celebration. Discuss whether students would prefer to arrange a coffeehouse or poetry reading or plan an exhibit of manuscripts.

c) Plan coffeehouse, reading, or display. Site selection. Physical setup. How to promote? Whom to invite? Scheduling. Hosting arrangements. Introductions and announcements. Sequence of events. Refreshments. Cleanup. Thank-you notes.

Homework: Prepare a poem for reading or display at the coffeehouse. Select that poem, or another, for the portfolio!

Poetry Event #1
Week 7. Occasional Poems

a) Discuss response to poetry event #1. Suggestions for a follow-up?

b) Plan a field trip to generate new poems. A visit to the local museum, a cultural or sporting event, a hike or a picnic.

c) Discuss the "poet's tools" to take on the field trip (all five or six senses plus notepad and writing implement).

d) The field trip.

Homework: Develop a poem from your field-trip notes. This poem looks at the occasion, and investigates some specific aspect of it: An ode to the bus driver? A reflection on the big maple under which some students ate their lunch? A comment on the place visited or a description of that place?

Week 8. Line Breaks

a) Read and discuss homework.

b) Discuss line breaks and how they are determined by rhythm/rhyme/enjambment/syllabic pattern, physical shape, and so forth (see Chapter 6).

c) Write a poem where all the lines are the same length on the page, a virtual rectangle.

d) Read and discuss.

Homework: Revise the poem to a syllabic pattern.

Week 9. Found Poetry

a) Read and discuss homework. In what ways do syllabics help or interfere? What do syllabics teach us about the language? What variety of syllabic patterns might one explore?

b) Show examples of found poems (see Chapter 5).

c) Distribute pages from newspapers.

d) Students start work on found poems.

Homework: Students complete their found poems or start new ones.

Week 10. Prose Poems

a) Read and discuss found poems.

b) Prose poems. Show examples, including "The Sandman" (Chapter 1) and "Control" (Chapter 5). What is each poem's attitude? How are those attitudes conveyed? Are any conventions violated?

c) Compose three prose poems in three five-minute sessions. The first poem should describe the room where the writer is seated; the second poem should be a description of a favorite place to be alone; and the third poem should describe a setting that brings out a reader's fears.

d) Read and discuss prose poems.

Homework: Revise and expand one of the three prose poems. Might it be revised into syllabic or rhythmic lines?

Week 11. Rhythm and Meter

a) Read and discuss prose poems. Think about point of view, attitude, parts of speech, departures from convention, and so on.

b) Discuss rhythm and meter—the limerick. Show examples of limericks. Discuss rhythm and rhyme scheme.

c) Write clean limericks. Try creating a serious limerick.

Homework: Polish limericks and create a sequence of limerick-stanzas.

Week 12. Story Poems

    a) Read and discuss limericks.

    b) Plan poetry event #2—a reading, coffeehouse, or display.

    c) Story poems. Show examples of Edward Field, Lucille Clifton, Naomi Shihab Nye poems. Discuss voice and attitude.

Homework: Write a first draft of a story poem. Make notes to explain the setting in which you write this poem. If music is playing, does its rhythm or melody play a role in the writing?

Poetry Event #2
Week 13. The Quatrain

    a) Read and discuss story poems.

    b) Discuss quatrains. Show examples.

    c) Write quatrains in cooperative groups—what variety of moods can be created? Can two or more quatrains be joined to form collaborative poems?

    d) Read and discuss quatrains: What are the advantages and drawbacks of collaboration?

Homework: Polish quatrains, join them with others to create a sequence or a longer poem.

Week 14. The Sonnet

    a) Read and discuss homework.

    b) Discuss the transitional strategies used to join some of the quatrains.

    c) Introduce the sonnet as a group of three quatrains with a two-line conclusion. Show examples. Look for the fulcrum in each poem.

Homework: Draft a sonnet.

Week 15. Metaphor/Simile

    a) Read and discuss sonnets. Find the fulcrum in each poem.

b) Review poems in your portfolio, identifying the fulcrums.

c) Discuss metaphor and simile.

d) Create examples of true metaphor.

Homework: Rewrite a poem from the portfolio with emphasis on the fulcrum and adding metaphor. Or create a new poem with a strong sense of fulcrum and metaphor.

Week 16. Review

a) Review the assignments and strategies discussed to date.

b) Write definitions of poetry.

c) Discuss personal goals for the next fourteen weeks.

Homework: Write a poem (free choice).

Week 17. Metaphor Hunt

a) Read and discuss homework. Which of the strategies discussed in the first sixteen weeks does each piece use?

b) Discuss and plan poetry event #3.

Homework: Metaphor hunt.

Week 18. Meter

a) Read and discuss metaphors found for homework.

b) Brainstorm new, one- or two-word topics under headings such as: Something I can't do; A place I'll never visit; An object used in a hoax; Favorite foods; Bad habits.

c) Meter: Revisit the limerick, then discuss the meter of "Stopping by Woods on a Snowy Evening." What is the difference between anapest and iambic pentameter? Can most of Robert Frost's poems be sung to the tune of "Hernando's Hideway" or "Yellow Rose of Texas"?

d) Practice reading Frost poems aloud to downplay or modify the rhythm.

Homework: Practice reading a Frost poem.

Poetry Event #3
Week 19. Longer Poems

a) Brief reading and discussion of Frost poems.

b) Review and discuss poetry event #3.

c) Distribute collections of longer poems. Note: When students are not staring at identical texts, their sense of discovery is heightened—borrow the entire poetry shelf from your school library and hand out the books, instructing students to look for longer poems!

d) Read and discuss favorites after skimming. What strategies are evident? Do messages come through?

Homework: Write a long poem using a favorite strategy.

Week 20. Villanelle

a) Read and discuss homework.

b) Discuss repetition and its use in villanelle (see Chapter 4).

c) Alone or in groups, students generate iambic pentameter couplets and write them on the board.

d) Each student writes a first draft villanelle, using couplets from the board at will.

e) Read and discuss first draft villanelles.

Homework: Polish villanelles.

Week 21. Mood and Voice

a) Read and discuss villanelles.

b) Mood and voice: Discuss the imperative, declarative, and interrogative moods. Discuss passive and active voice.

c) Write a collaborative poem (see Chapter 3) with a variety of moods and voices.

d) Read and discuss.

Homework: Polish or write new poem with a variety of moods and voices.

Week 22. Person and Number

a) Read and discuss homework.

b) Discuss *person* and *number*. Conduct a brief drill to ensure that all students understand the differences between first, second, third person as well as singular and plural.

c) Create list poems that demonstrate a variety of persons. (I see her on the shoreline./ She edges one toe into the ocean./ He is like a jealous child, pretending not to notice.// At dinner, no one speaks:/ We pretend that nothing is wrong.)

d) Read and discuss multiperson list poems.

e) Review mood, voice, person, and number. Experiment to see how existing, declarative mood poems might be altered by revision into the imperative mood. (See her on the shoreline,/ how she edges one toe into the ocean./ Be a jealous child, pretend not to notice.// Don't speak at dinner:/ Pretend nothing is wrong.) What are the varieties of intensity that can be implied with imperative mood? ("Grant me the wisdom . . ." "Please give me a dime"; "Please give me the money"; "Give me the money!")

Homework: Write a new poem that uses the imperative mood extensively (recipe or prayer poems).

Week 23. Concrete Poetry

a) Read and discuss imperative poems.

b) Distribute (handouts or overhead projector?) and discuss examples of concrete poems.

c) Write concrete poems.

d) Read, show, and discuss concrete poems.

Homework: Write new concrete poems.

Week 24. Current Events

a) Read, show, and discuss concrete poems.

b) Current events in poetry. Define and brainstorm current events.

c) Write poems related to current events.

d) Read and discuss.

e) Plan and discuss poetry event #4.

Homework: Polish or research and draft a new current events poem.

Poetry Event #4
Week 25. Themes

a) Read and discuss current events poems.

b) Discuss poetry event #4 and plan final celebration.

c) Discuss themes. History, science, science fiction, and so on.

d) From what class other than this one can you extract a theme for a poem?

e) Begin drafting a poem for another class.

Homework: Complete theme poem.

Week 26. Adapting Existing Forms: The Sestina

a) Read and discuss theme poems.

b) Explain the sestina, and show examples (see Chapter 5).

c) Strategies for "adapting" a form.

d) Draft sestinas or quatrinas.

Homework: Revise and polish draft poems.

Week 27. Breaking the Rules

a) Read and discuss sestinas and quatrinas.

b) Breaking the rules: Distribute examples of poems where rules are broken or conventions are violated. "Grammar and punctuation are a courtesy to the reader." What benefits and problems result from neglecting this courtesy?

c) Draft poems that break the rules.

d) Read and discuss.

Homework: Draft and photocopy new poems that break rules.

Week 28. "Bad" Poetry

a) Read and discuss homework.

b) What makes poems "good"? List qualities on the board. What makes poems "bad"? List on board.

c) Write poems that are intentionally "bad."

d) Read and discuss "bad" poems.

e) Discuss and plan final celebration.

Homework: Try writing a "good" poem, possibly by revising a "bad" one.

Week 29. Field Trip

a) Read and discuss homework.

b) Discuss and plan culminating field trip.

c) Culminating field trip.

Homework: Occasional Poem: Write a poem generated by the field trip.

Week 30. Review Portfolios

a) Read and discuss homework. What strategies from weeks past are evident in each poem?

b) Review portfolios and select favorite poem.

c) Reading and discussion of favorite poems from portfolio.

Final Celebration!

No curriculum, no gathering of prescriptive advice, no set of special exercises can equal the power of a teacher who writes with the students. Teacher participation, roughly equal to the amount of focus given any student, provides the key to transforming the classroom into a writers' community. Once community has been established, writers start to feel inspired by the fact that, often for the first time in their lives, they have a real audience for their work. Ideally, it's an audience that encourages risk taking, experimentation, careful observation, thoughtful word choice, and honesty.

When these qualities infuse a person's writing, I pay attention for what I might learn. The year has many days, so I have many days to say, with truth: "Today, you are my favorite poet."

Appendix
Six Poems, Six Exercises

1. Twist the Knife

Passing Thru

You see them at truckstops, signs that litter the walls,
Work fascinates me I can sit & watch it for hours, Plan
    Ahea
And the waitress so sullen you want to tip extra just to
    show her
How wrong she was about you, her white dress with lit-
    tle bumps
All over the material making it look almost gray and
    you see thru
To the bra doing its thin job and she wants you to pay up
So she can go home, saunters over and yawns between
    chews "Youthru?"
And not to be mean but because you're lonely you ask
    for another donut:
She extends it with aluminum pincers so it seems
    germproof
But you watched earlier when she emptied the bakery
    cellophane damn near
Fondling each one as if here at least was something she
    cared for

And licking all the extra sugar off her fingers at the end.

"To hell with aluminum—let's dance!" you cry and twist her hand
Over the counter so she drops pincers and your donut
"Hey cut that out whatsa matter with you you crazy or somethin:
    Joe!"
And she starts yelling but you've already passed thru
That critical tunnel where you decide:
"This is a dream, I'll do what I please"
And one of the truckers looks up from the coffee he stirred with his
    eyes
As you think of your mother who told you about them and how
    one
would kill you someday just like they got your father

And you dance with her back and forth over the countertop
Until Joe comes out at which point the trucker gets involved too
And both of them have you by the legs and the waitress is saying
"Wise guy wise guy" over and over
And the donut and the pincers are on the floor
And if you wanna know more go do it yourself.

I could never have written this poem and several others that came after it if I had not read Donald Hall's "Ode to a Waterfowl," which, in its final lines, addresses the reader directly in a surprisingly harsh manner. I call this a "twist the knife" poem.

Write a poem where the reader is led through a series of humorous images and is sharing the joke with the author or is otherwise lulled into agreeing with what appears to be the poet's point of view. Then, in the final lines, turn the tables on the reader. The poem's fulcrum will probably be found just before the poem starts to twist the knife.

2. Memoir

Eagle Rock

Remember us to Eagle Rock
Billy Koenig & me at 9 years apiece
hiking one Saturday in early May
way up past the house with half a pack
of embezzled cigarettes & enough matches

to light each one a dozen times,

Remember us to Eagle Rock
where couples in their cars
pulled off the road to watch the N.Y. skyline
& make love as Billy & me
dizzy from tobacco sitting on the big pavilion
of the castle with its stoned out windows
wondering what to do once we felt better

And how as if we had no choice
we'd find ourselves each time
working toward the place the cars were parked
provided by the town, a pressure seal
for lovers prevented by circumstance
from doing it at home

And picture Koenig & me, pockets stuffed
with newly sprouted acorns
we used to stone the lovers
I can't believe we stoned the lovers
taking such liberties with our health
& how, when we did get chased

we'd run & run & run
half laughing & half very scared
some wild-yelling cursing half-dressed
passion victim in pursuit
I hated to trip but often did
Billy usually way ahead of me, down down
into the forest below Eagle Rock
to a cave we knew where
we'd heave & choke & get our breath,
lungs aching from the cigarettes & from the chase
& laugh & swear we'd never come so close
to getting caught

For many poets, the richest sources of material lie in their childhood memories. For me, at least, these memories often involve behavior that was not appreciated by adult society. Not that I was a bad boy, but many of my memoir poems touch on common types of childhood malfeasance. A story involving wrongful acts is usually more interesting than one describing the narrator's virtues.

Write a poem that re-creates an event without analyzing it, allowing the reader to draw the conclusions. The event does not need to involve a moment of naughtiness, nor does it need to be autobiographical: one may choose to create fiction in this exercise!

3. Natural Habits

The Ruffed Grouse

That distant, stalling, motor-like, low-pitched thrum
is Mr. Ruffed Grouse somewhere near a nuptial thicket.
Where he goes with his drums in May
she understands, left still, hoping

to pass for the colors of broken limbs,
duller even than the dozen eggs she keeps.
Every day I happen by, eyes working hard
to find her in the shadowed nest

before she leaves the eggs and tries her ritual
lead him away from the nest
and when the young are hatched some morning
by evening she will have led them off too

Given that we are the only animal that we do not recognize as an animal, I am often impressed by the similarities between our habits and those found in nature. In this sense human nature is not an oxymoron, but a redundancy! In "The Ruffed Grouse," I hope the reader sees a parallel between the behavior of the male ruffed grouse and deadbeat dads.

Write a poem that, investigating the habits of some nonhuman creature, implies the behavior of at least some humans. Brainstorming a list of nonhuman creatures may help some students. Pack rat, predator, worm, and so forth. Did you know that some anthropologists think of the engagement ring as the human equivalent of the large bug or piece of grain some species of male birds present to their prospective mates as a way of proving their capacity to be good providers to the hoped-for nestlings? When males of the nonhuman wild fight for the opportunity to mate with a desirable female, is nature providing for the best possible natural selection?

4. Cookbook Poems

Recipe

What will you feed your future dinner?
Liquid seaweed.
                    You'll feed it liquid seaweed.
This is 99 cents for four liquid ounces, so make it go far
by watering down at a ratio of 1-600.
(Make sure the one part is the liquid seaweed.)

Now you got yourself a thriving plant,
what you going to do with it?
Out on the windowsill but bring in at dusk
or whenever the nights threaten to go below freezing.
(Here that means you need a lot of indoor space,
especially if you're bringing the peas and potatoes in each night.)
When danger of frost is past, set plant out in garden,
pluck away weeds and try not to water. Let the roots grow deep
in search of greater moisture and warmth
than fickle human caring, the occasional hose
or the equally fickle uncaring of the heavens, can provide:
let it be, but keep the weeds away.

What will you feed your future dinner?
Give it green cow manure or whatever you can find
that helps add bulk to the earth,
not just little pellets from the factories.
Your soil needs stuff, not quick jolts
of speed that rob it of vitality.

Take tomato plants that have fought and gone leggy
for the little light that makes it through your window,
and lay roots and stem horizontal in a trench,
two inches deep, cover with potting soil and heap good green cow
    dung
on top to make a mound.
                    Do this in full sunshine then run for cover
you got spaghetti sauce dripping from the clouds
tomatoes exploding from the earth
like the wildest dreams of Generals.
Bubbling earth, we treasure

your bounty, your visual possibility, the glory
of our cooking spread beyond political borders,
geographical zones erased, television flattening all terrain
great waves of radio and inhumanity
baking in the polar stew.

Excuse this digression. You gotta believe
there's gonna be a September to start reading this recipe anyway.
So you take the plant and keep its roots moist and warm
and feed it until it starts feeding you
or the raccoons:
a subject of great interest. Don't shoot
raccoons, don't try to fence them out.
Don't tie your biggest dog to the garden fence
because raccoons will kill it.
And don't try to wave them off once they know the corn's aripening.

Surround your corn with a field of cucumbers,
or failing that at least a band of them, four feet thick,
and space four paper cups filled with beer in the cucumber bed
and outside of that stake human hair
in those airy nets that once held onions,
and turn a transistor radio tuned to a wild all night disco station
in a plastic sack to protect it from rain
up full volume every night at sundown.
Raccoons won't want to dance to all that music,
amid the spiny vines of the cucumber patch
and will assume the flat, tepid cups of beer
are all that remains of a bad party. Don't ask me
what role the human hair plays,
though I cannot recommend this scheme without it.

The pot is set to boiling before you go out for the harvest.
Likewise, before I go fishing, I chill my favorite chablis
and build the fire, for the fish
just jump
into my hands and I wrestle them, like my vegetables
back to the waiting fire,
stoked more by hunger, imagination, than by nuclear fuels or hard-
    wood,
the fire that drives the germs away, the fire that tenderizes,
the fire for which this recipe's prepared.

The imperative mood can be a powerful tool in writing, especially because it addresses the reader directly and because it has such a dynamic range, from outright demand ("Give me the money!") to humble prayer ("Give me the grace"). The imperative mood can go much further than "Recipe" does in adding urgency, humility, authority, or hostility to an event or situation.

Write a poem where the imperative mood is dominant. This might be a poem for two voices, perhaps the voices of a parent and child, or a police officer and a criminal.

5. Reversing the Rules

Wrestling to Lose

None of us were winners, like
Armentrout or Beebe, the heavyweight
who surprised opponents twice his size
in the Unlimited Division, flipping one
who still scowled from the peevish handshake
that had to start each match.

Spring Weekend my parents drove my date up from New Jersey
and I wrestled the 135 pounder from Peddie
who took 30 seconds to pin me Spring Weekend
the year before. My father
clapped my back in the locker room
and pronounced it "a moral victory."

Behind the gym two weeks later
the hacks on the team smoked their first cigarettes
since fall and chafed at the gung hoes
who were still running laps. Where are they now?
Well, Armentrout's big in business for sure,
and Beebe's a famous neurosurgeon!

And us hackers? I'll hazard our wages
per capita can't touch *theirs*. We were artists,
idealists, the boys who invented wrestling to lose:
slam yourself down on the mat. With shoulders flat
hold your opponent just three seconds over you
helpless in the victory pose.

My brother told me of a version of backgammon he and a friend play where the object of the game is to lose. I took this idea and applied it to a physical competition. Preventing one's opponent from lying, shoulders flat, on the gymnasium floor might provide as aggressive a wrestling match as one that observed the traditional rules. What other types of reversed-rules competition might a poet imagine? What about a war? A political campaign? A baking competition? A watermelon-eating contest? Think of a country fair, and all the blue ribbons that are awarded.

Brainstorm a list of the many human endeavors for which prizes are awarded, then write a poem where all competitors are trying to win last place.

6. History

Moment

They say Anwar refused to duck, stood in defiance,
"His Last Lesson to Us" claims
an aide who lives to talk, and tried to pull
> the great man
> down to safety.
He stood to take it,
knowing it inevitable,
must have planned
> when it comes, their hatred
> can take my body
> but not my spirit.
I will never cower.
Better they should work their will.

He wouldn't sit down!
Because someone wanted him dead
bad enough, did his
own guards turn their backs or
threaten the cameramen from ABC? Stop the cameras!
How many had this wish he accommodated by standing?
Who says great man of peace
who says detested traitorous scorpion?

Sitting fat with no one caring except the immediate family
all we have to duck are low transoms, excessive taxation,
starvation and cold, the occasional nut who'll violate anybody
for a splash on the local news. Makes you want to be anonymous,

determined to creep around unnoticed, unthreatened.
Ever since 18½ minutes at Kent State,
ever since John Lennon caught Chapman's gunfire
and Anwar in review of his weapons
taught us to greet the moment when we, made careless
by longevity, stand to meet the bullets
in mid-air, or when as horrible
we wake to breathe the dust we know
will slowly do us in.

Like memoir, historical events provide a rich store of topics for poems. From trivial to tragic, they present an opportunity to explore both fact and nuance, then to extend it, if desired, into the future. In "Moment," I used the newspaper accounts of the assassination of Anwar Sadat, then extended the possible intimidation one might feel upon learning of violence against people who are leaders. As for nuance, I used this poem to hint that the famous 18½-minute "gap" in Nixon's White House tapes obliterated the planning of violent action against antiwar student protesters. Far-fetched? Sure, but it's as plausible a theory as any regarding what the President's secretary erased from those tapes!

To write historical poems, students can comb newspapers or their history texts for possible topics. Current events often have more emotional pull than events from the past, so be sure the students know they can link ancient history to recent news, possibly in a fashion similar to that of a poet who implies similarities between the habits of nonhuman creatures and the human animal.

Works Cited

Ammons, A. R. 1965. *Tape for the Turn of the Year*. Ithaca, NY: Cornell University Press.

Carruth, Hayden. 1996. *Selected Essays and Reviews*. Port Townsend, WA: Copper Canyon Press.

———. 1978. *Brothers, I Loved You All*. Riverdale-on-Hudson, NY: The Sheep Meadow Press.

———, ed. 1970. *The Voice That Is Great Within Us*. New York: Bantam Books.

Ciardi, John, and Miller Williams. 1975. *How Does a Poem Mean?* Boston: Houghton Mifflin.

Clifton, Lucille. 1987. *Next: New Poems*. Rochester, NY: BOA Editions.

Cole, William, ed. 1973. *Poems One Line & Longer*. New York: Grossman Publishers.

Feldman, Claire. 1997. *Hewitt's House*. Middlebury, VT: Self-published.

Field, Edward. 1987. *New and Selected Poems*. Riverdale-on-Hudson, NY: The Sheep Meadow Press.

Hewitt, Geof. 1995. *A Portfolio Primer*. Portsmouth, NH: Heinemann.

Janeczko, Paul, ed. 1985. *Pocket Poems*. New York: Bradbury Press.

Lester, Julius. 1969. *Search for the New Land: History as Subjective Experience*. New York: Doubleday.

Marquis, Don. 1970. *Archie and Mehitabel*. New York: Doubleday.

Morice, Dave. 1994. *More Poetry Comics.* Chicago: a capella books.

———. 1983. *How to Make Poetry Comics.* New York: Teachers & Writers Collaborative.

Nye, Naomi Shihab, and Paul B. Janeczko, eds. 1996. *I Feel a Little Jumpy Around You.* New York: Simon & Schuster.

Nye, Naomi Shihab. 1992. *This Same Sky,* ed. New York: Four Winds Press.

Padgett, Ron, ed. 1987. *Handbook of Poetic Forms.* New York: Teachers & Writers Collaborative.

Ray, David. 1965. *X-Rays.* Ithaca, NY: Cornell University Press.

Rief, Linda. 1992. *Seeking Diversity.* Portsmouth, NH: Heinemann.

Bibliography

Carruth, Hayden. 1996. *Selected Essays & Reviews.* Port Townsend, WA: Copper Canyon Press.

——, ed. 1970. *The Voice That Is Great Within Us.* New York: Bantam Books.

Ciardi, John, and Miller Williams. 1975. *How Does a Poem Mean?* Boston: Houghton Mifflin.

Collom, Jack. 1985. *Moving Windows: Evaluating the Poetry Children Write.* New York: Teachers & Writers Collaborative.

de Paola, Tomie. 1985. *Mother Goose.* New York: G.P. Putnam's Sons.

Edgar, Christopher, and Ron Padgett, eds. 1995. *Old Faithful: 18 Writers Present Their Favorite Writing Assignments.* New York: Teachers & Writers Collaborative.

Field, Edward. 1987. *New and Selected Poems.* Riverdale-on-Hudson, NY: The Sheep Meadow Press.

Graves, Donald H., and Bonnie S. Sunstein, eds. 1992. *Portfolio Portraits:* Heinemann.

Hewitt, Geof. 1995. *A Portfolio Primer: Teaching, Collecting, and Assessing Student Writing.* Portsmouth, NH: Heinemann.

——. 1989. *Just Worlds.* Greenfield Center, NY: Ithaca House.

——, ed. 1972. *Living in Whales: Vermont Public School Stories and Poems.* Montpelier, VT: Vermont Council on the Arts.

——, ed. 1969. *Quickly Aging Here: Some Poets of the 1970s.* New York: Anchor Doubleday.

Kearns, Jane. 1997. *Where to Begin: A Guide to Teaching Secondary English.* Portsmouth, NH: Boynton/Cook.

King, Nancy. 1993. *Storymaking and Drama.* Portsmouth, NH: Heinemann.

Kowit, Steve. 1995. *In the Palm of Your Hand: The Poet's Portable Workshop.* Gardiner, ME: Tilbury House.

Lamott, Anne. 1994. *Bird by Bird: Some Instructions on Writing and Life.* New York: Anchor Doubleday.

Lane, Barry. 1993. *After THE END: Teaching and Learning Creative Revision.* Portsmouth, NH: Heinemann.

Lester, Julius. 1969. *Search for the New Land: History as Subjective Experience.* New York: Doubleday.

Lourie, Dick, and Mark Pawlak, eds. 1995. *Bullseye: Stories and Poems by Outstanding High School Writers.* Brooklyn, NY: Hanging Loose Press.

———, eds. 1989. *Smart Like Me: High School-Age Writing from the Sixties to Now.* Brooklyn, NY: Hanging Loose Press.

Morice, Dave. 1994. *More Poetry Comics.* Chicago: a capella books.

———. 1983. *How to Make Poetry Comics.* New York: Teachers & Writers Collaborative.

Murphy, Sandra, and Mary Ann Smith. 1995. *Writing Portfolios: A Bridge from Teaching to Assessment.* Ontario: Pippin, Markham.

Nye, Naomi Shihab, and Paul B. Janeczko, eds. 1996. *I Feel a Little Jumpy Around You.* New York: Simon & Schuster.

Nye, Naomi Shihab, ed. 1992. *This Same Sky: A Collection of Poems from Around the World.* New York: Four Winds Press.

Padgett, Ron. 1997. *Creative Reading.* Urbana, IL: National Council of Teachers of English.

———, ed. 1987. *Handbook of Poetic Forms.* New York: Teachers & Writers Collaborative.

Rief, Linda. 1992. *Seeking Diversity: Language Arts with Adolescents.* Portsmouth, NH: Heinemann.

Romano, Tom. 1987. *Clearing the Way: Working with Teenage Writers.* Portsmouth, NH: Heinemann.

Sears, Peter. 1990. *Gonna Bake Me a Rainbow Poem: A Student Guide to Writing Poetry.* New York: Scholastic.

———. 1986. *Secret Writing: Keys to the Mysteries of Reading and Writing.* New York: Teachers & Writers Collaborative.

Tsujimoto, Joseph I. 1988. *Teaching Poetry Writing to Adolescents.* Urbana, IL: National Council of Teachers of English.

Yancey, Kathleen Blake, ed. 1992. *Portfolios in the Writing Classroom.* Urbana, IL: National Council of Teachers of English.

Zemelman, Steven, and Harvey Daniels. 1988. *A Community of Writers Teaching Writing in the Junior and Senior High School.* Portsmouth, NH: Heinemann.

Periodicals

English Journal. National Council of Teachers of English, 1111 W. Kenyon Road, Urbana, IL, 61801.

Merlyn's Pen: The National Magazine of Student Writing. P.O. Box 1058, East Greenwich, RI, 02818.

Potato Hill Poetry Newsletter. 361 Watertown St., Newton, MA, 02158.

Teachers & Writers. Teachers & Writers Collaborative, 5 Union Square West, New York, NY, 10003.

The 21st Century. Box 30, Newton, MA, 02161. www.teenpaper.org